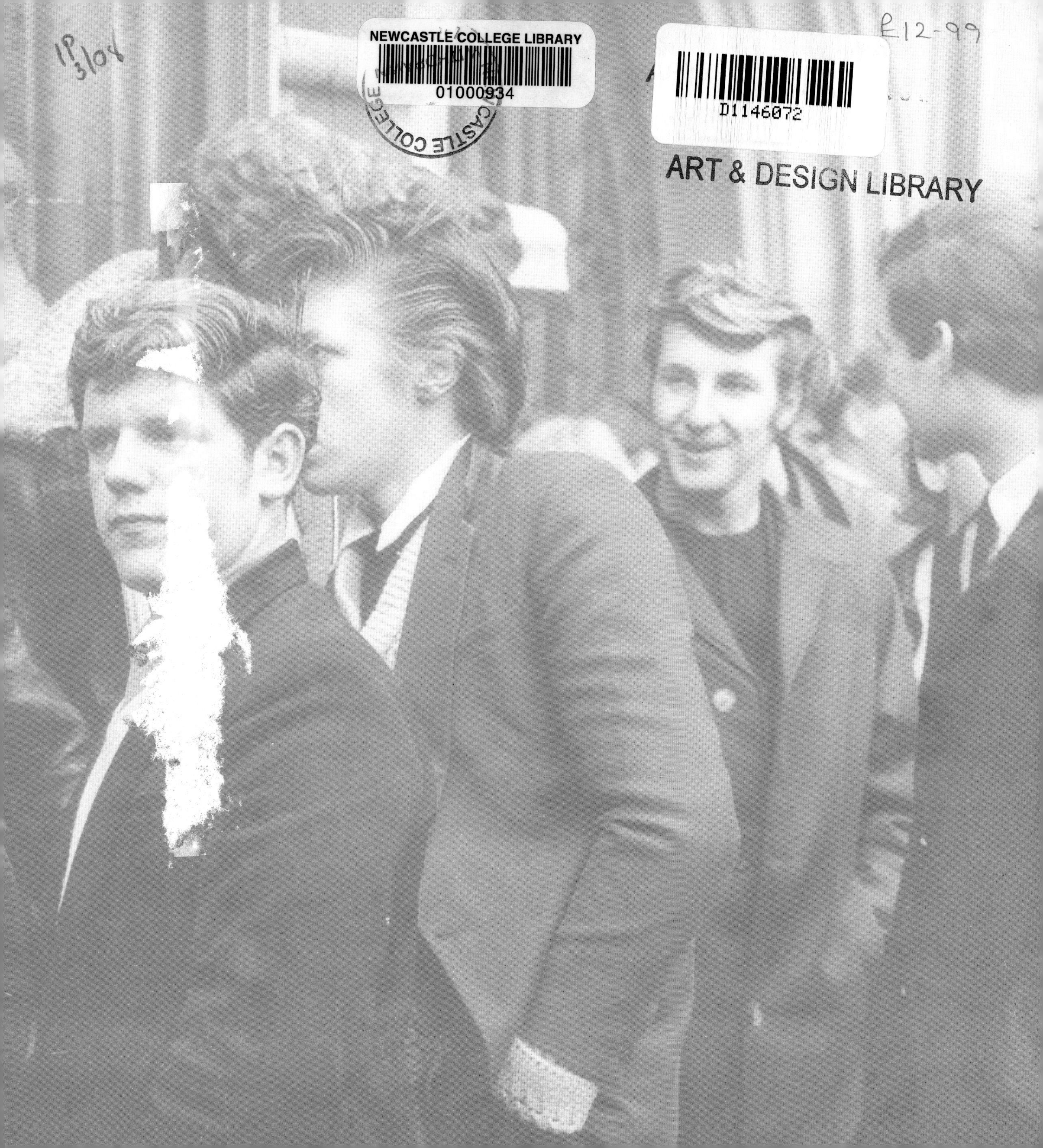

REBEL REBEL

25 YEARS OF TEENAGE TRAUMA
—— FROM DEAN TO THE DAMNED ——

CHRIS TARRANT

REBEL REBEL

25 YEARS OF TEENAGE TRAUMA
—— FROM DEAN TO THE DAMNED ——

CHRIS TARRANT

PYRAMID BOOKS

PYRAMID BOOKS

First published in 1991 by Pyramid Books, an imprint of Reed International
Books, Michelin House, 81 Fulham Road, London SW3 6RB

The Author's moral rights have been asserted.

ISBN 1 855 10087 8

Designed by Thumb Design Partnership
Produced by Mandarin Offset
Printed and bound in Hong Kong

CONTENTS

REBEL REBEL

'No one did anything for me. I don't owe anything to anyone. If I live to be a hundred there won't be time to do everything I want. My purpose in life does not include a hankering to charm society.'

So said Christopher Jehosophat Tarrant aged ten and thrée-quarters, pre-teenage hero, tough guy and all round right-on rebel.

Well, OK, actually it was James Dean, but I was just about to say it if only he hadn't butted in. History shows that Jimmy Dean didn't live to be a hundred, but I did, and most of us who grew up in the new affluence that young people enjoyed in the mid Fifties felt that for the first time the world was ours to kick around a bit.

Mum and Dad no longer had total control of our purse strings, even though nearly all young kids still lived at home, and it meant that for the first time a generation had the ability to choose where they went, who they went with and what they looked like when they got there.

In the decades that followed Hiroshima there was a real fear that the world might end at any minute, well inside four minutes, and a couple of times it very nearly did. We all grew up under the shadow of imminent apocalypse, and with a feeling that we wanted to have more of our share before we went.

The marketing men were ever so keen to help us of course.

The teenage market was as new as teenagers themselves, and with their disinclination to save a single penny and wanting to spend it *now,* teenagers were a very important and exploitable section of the public. Of course none of this was as clear at the time as it is in hindsight.

Our idea of rebelling in the Fifties was often simply saying 'Do I really HAVE to, Dad?', usually followed by a firm 'YES YOU DO', followed at our end by a reluctant 'OK then...I'll do it at once'. Pretty pathetic really, but at least you felt you'd tried. Hardly Daniel Cohn-Bendit, but not bad for ten and three-quarters.

All we wanted was a little bit of identity. Until Bill Haley and company, kids always dressed like school kids, then they dressed like grown-ups, suits and ties, brown suits at that....we did that till we were about a hundred and ninety, and then we died. Then you were free to wear what you liked.

Just coming home late and climbing in through the bedroom window could seem subversive in the Fifties. Donning a Dean-ish scowl or mustering a Marlon mumble was enough to make you feel a bit like you were kicking against something, even if it was only the wall outside your house. The good thing about post-war building techniques was that the house almost certainly wouldn't fall down.

For most of us in the next few years, it wasn't being naughty that mattered it was being seen to look as if we were naughty. We were rebels 'cos we told people we were, and that was all we needed.

Many a Sixties teenage drug fiend got high just lighting a joss stick; the Revolution began and ended in most cases with a Che Guevara poster on the bedroom wall, and even the shock tactics of the punks often amounted to no more than dyed hair, triple pierced ears and a stick-on swastika tattoo.

So much of adolescent outrage turned out to be really no more than hype and image, feeding on our need to belong to something, anything, that the Establishment didn't approve of. So, when the Beatles became accepted by Mums, and even the occasional Dad (though certainly not mine, Basil 'Bing Will Always Be King' Tarrant), we dropped them like hot potatoes and went off in search of something altogether more hideous, unlovable and evil

smelling. Thank God Mick Jagger and Keith Richards were there when we needed them.

For so many of us, whichever fad we chose was really just a weekend off from the rest of our life. You could be a Hippy from Friday rush hour until the spectacular sunrise over Stonehenge of a Monday morning, but you'd still be driving home at tea time

as an estate agent, man. And a lot of the punk hairdos you saw in the Seventies were wash-outable; every Sunday night, they had to go, along with the stick-on safety pins through the nose, back in the bedroom drawer till next Friday.

If this all sounds a bit cynical, that's only because regrettably it is.

The saddest programme I ever saw in my life was an American TV documentary 'Woodstock - 21 Years On'. It was a then-and-now look at the hippies who dominated that extraordinary event. Long flowing locks, kaftans, flowers in their hair, psychedelic painted faces, 'Make Love Not War' - they had it all. But the Sixties footage was cut together with interviews with the same people twenty-one years later. They were unrecognisable. They were fat, they were bald, they were chartered accountants, they were real estate investors. This was depressing enough, but far more upsetting was their unanimous condemnation of every single thing the hippies stood for. Now at the age of 43, they'd discovered that the real point of their being placed on this planet was to sell condominiums to little old blue rinsed ladies in Fort Lauderdale, and that 'Give Peace A Chance' and 'Make Love Not War' was all a moment of childish madness. I still think that making love is infinitely preferable to making war, although I'm no longer sure which is more likely to cause your early departure from this life.

We rebelled, we argued, we fell out with our Mums and Dads. We were asked never to darken their doorstep again, but you knew, or at least you hoped you knew, that they didn't really mean it. And as you stormed off into the night wishing them a happy rest of the century, you didn't mean it either. It got bloody freezing at about half past two in the morning.

Teenage traumas have always been about breaking taboos - a smoke behind the bike sheds, a hurried grope in the back row of the pictures and that first awful 'technicolour yawn' that put you off drink for weeks.

We're all teenagers at heart, and armchair anarchists I suspect, so these recollections of revolting youth from Johnnie Ray to Johnny Rotten should evoke warm memories - and the odd embarrassed blush - in anyone over thirtysomething going-on-sixteen.

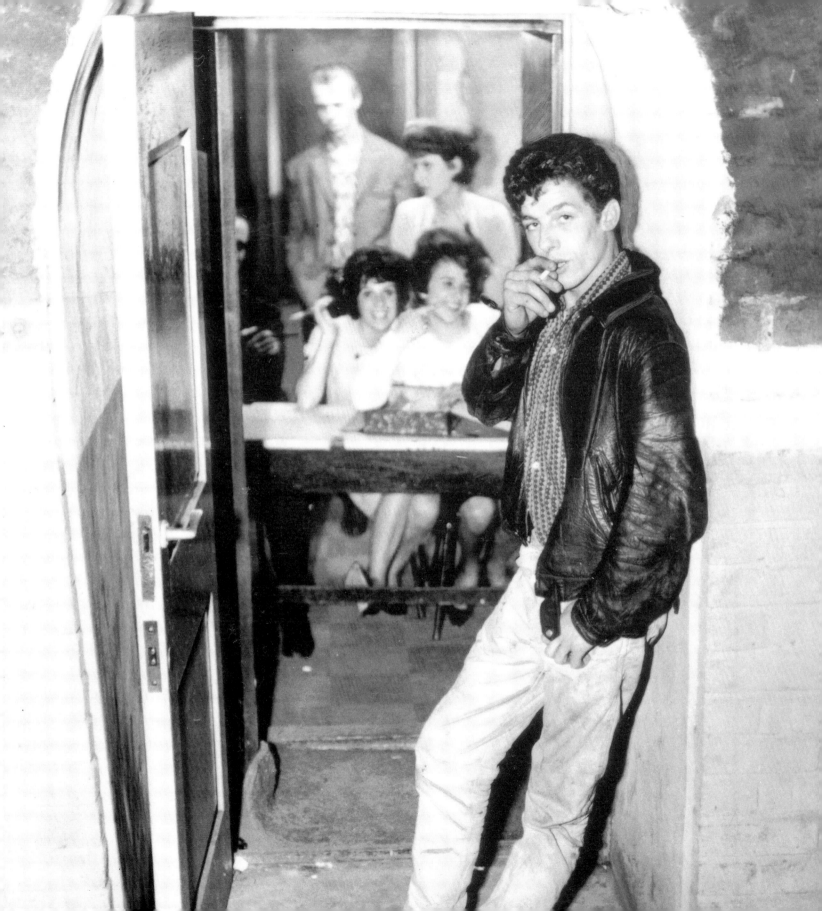

50s

REBELS WITHOUT A CAUSE

Judy Ford from Macclesfield was never a teenager - they didn't exist when she was young:

> *At the start of the Fifties we were children until the day we started work, then we were adults, no between stage.*

Mean, moody or just manipulated? For the first time there was an image to live up to.

If there had been no such thing as teenagers, it would have been necessary to invent them. And at the start of the Fifties, there wasn't, so they did.

I mean, those demob suits after the War looked alright in Humphrey Bogart films but were hardly the cat's whiskers ten years later, and the dodgy black market nylons the girls bought off the spivs weren't much better.

So, once the call-up was cancelled and they were picking their pimples in civvy street instead of the Army, with a job and money in their pockets - 'You've never had it so good' bleated Harold Macmillan - they seemed perfect suckers for the big sell.

Things never go as simply as planned. Like Frankenstein's monster, once the teenager had been created there was no telling what mayhem was in store for everyone...

JEEPERS CREEPERS

The first statement of the newly-emergent teenager was in what he or she wore - indeed, fashion-to-shock has been the prime badge of teen rebellion ever since. And it didn't take much to shock in the early Fifties.

The Teddy Boys came first. Contrary to myth, they appeared a year or two before the arrival of rock'n'roll. So called because of the 'Edwardian' cut of the clothes (ironically one of the most straight-laced and conformist of eras) - velvet collars on long draped jackets, with narrow 'drainpipe' trousers - the style was launched by smart Saville Row tailors for the Hooray Henrys of the day before being nicked by the lower orders in dance halls and billiard saloons up and down the country.

Amid incredible press hysteria, the Teds were blamed for every kind of juvenile delinquency, from cinema seat-slashing to mugging old ladies, though most of the time they seemed to be hanging round fairly harmlessly and mindlessly on street corners and in coffee bars like all the

Right at the beginning of the decade, even the most modest diversion was an event to look forward to, as D. Lappin of Middleton, near Manchester, recalls:

Sunday night was when it all happened...it started about 3 o'clock when you met your mates in the local Temperance Bar, and over a hot Bovril the evening's visit to the cinema was planned. This meant a walk of over a mile to Manchester as the Middleton picture houses weren't allowed to open on Sundays. Afterwards we had the long walk back..all the boys walked on one side of the road, the girls on the other - unless you had 'clicked'. Most of us ended up back at the Temperance Bar for a quick drink, a listen to the juke box, then home. If you were lucky enough to borrow the family radio you could listen in bed to the 'Top Ten Tunes' which were still based on sheet music sales in those days.

It wasn't cheap keeping up appearances, as Jack Warner of Romford remembers:

By the time you'd bought the suit, got a haircut and put away enough money for Saturday night there was nothing left. You had to scrounge a bit off the old man or go hungry during your dinner break for the next week.

...though Albert Hughes found a way of making extra pocket money:

Sweets, butter and a few other things were still 'on the ration' early in the Fifties, so there was a good black market if you could get your hands on it....a few pounds of margarine or a piece of boiled ham, all worth a few bob. We were the last of the spivs I suppose, like the 'wide boys' who flourished after the War.

other teenagers. So just to don 14"-bottom 'drainies' or 'brothel creepers' (sorry 'beetle crushers') was deemed rebellious in itself.

Likewise, Teddy Girl fashion was outlawed by most 'respectable' parents, especially the more flagrant extremes like waist-hugging waspie belts, tight sweaters and short (i.e. kneelength!) skirts.

BLUEJEAN BOP

Most of the rest of teen togs were pure Americana, inspired by the cinema and its new youthful heart-throbs James Dean and Marlon Brando - before he stuffed his mouth with cotton wool. Bluejeans, leather jackets, T-shirts, sun glasses even in the pouring rain, and baseball boots (trainers before their time) - all innocuous enough, but in the eyes of Fifties parents part of a creeping Americanism that was rather flash and therefore suspect, along with chewing gum, jukeboxes and incomprehensible music called rock'n'roll.

Reinforced by the rock'n'rollers - denims and biker jackets have remained the two enduring items of young fashion to this day. Both early examples of unisex (a radical notion if ever there was one), the leather jacket in particular became a universal cipher for youthful revolt. All you needed was an old flying jacket, a defiant snarl and a blob of Brylcreem and you'd be fighting off the birds. The initial and most celebrated leather-clad anti-hero was Marlon Brando as a delinquent biker in 'The Wild One'- pure image of course as the actual film was banned from British screens until 1967! His reply to the question 'What are you rebelling against, Johnny?', 'Whad'ya got?', inspired a whole generation of would-be rebels.

MARY'S LITTLE SHOP

While the boys were trying to look mean and macho the girls, at least by the end of the decade, were toying with the idea of discarding their conical Maidenform bras. Mary Quant was their saviour. By 1959 the about-to-become-mind-bogglingly-wealthy Mary had opened her second shop, Bazaar in Chelsea. The idea was to offer 'a bouillabaisse of clothes and accessories', bright and affordable and, ideally, shocking to the older generation. She was about to revolutionise the whole convention of the catwalk by not using the standard debs delights in whalebone corsets who walked as if they had toffee between their thighs. Instead Quant used top photographic models from a new generation of glossy magazines. Forgetting the usual tedious commentary of 'Tallulah is wearing an enchanting little number made entirely out of gold lamé, hessian and cabbage stalks.....' Mary sent out her vivacious young models strutting and pouting to the sound of blaring pop music.

KISS CURLS 'N' QUIFFS

The Fifties saw some epic hairstyles; the Bill Haley Kiss Curl - basically you took a tuft of hair from the front of your head, smeared it with chip fat and plastered it down over one eyebrow - not very alluring, even at the time; the Brando, with a ringletted fringe pioneered by Marlon which in latter years looked a damn sight better on Bonnie Langford; and of course the Teddy Boys' DA - DA as in duck's arse, because that's exactly what it looked like from the rear, with a quiff dripping with Brylcreem sweeping across the front. An even more extreme example of the quiff was a phallic monstrosity known as the Elephant's Trunk (Indian or African, depending on the size of your ears), while the Tony Curtis was a curly-top variation named after the Hollywood star.

Fifteen in 1958, Jean Ringland of Wythenshawe was a 'typical Teddy Girl':

I wore a white 'scooter' or 'autograph' jacket, so called because one always hoped someone famous would sign them. They were only made of white plastic but I thought I was really hip in mine. I had a black pencil skirt with a slit up the back to show a bit of leg, and a spotted cotton blouse that cost me 4s 6d. My lipstick cost 1s 6d and was called something like Frosted Pink. It was so pale it made me look ill, but it was all the rage so I wore it. My hair was cut in a DA, and to complete the outfit I wore black slip-on shoes and luminous lime green or orange socks.

As well as getting a Brando or a Boston at the barber's, you could pick up racing tips, the latest jokes and, if you dared, 'something for the weekend'.

Girls are wearing jeans and sneakers like their US counterparts, while boys' hair seems to be growing longer by the day - soon you won't be able to tell them apart.

Equally annoying to parents, teachers and employers was the Crew Cut - so therefore a viable option. Again essentially American, it took the good old British military 'short back and sides' recommended by Dads everywhere to a typically transatlantic extreme.

Plus of course there were the Beatniks, with the first really long hair since the Iron Age - at least we thought it was pretty long-haired at the time, today they'd probably look about as unkempt and shaggy as John Major.

But be it quiffs or kiss curls, all this teenage tonsorial flamboyance was swept under the regimental barber's chair for wimps and wild ones alike who were caught in the net of National Service.

John Patterson, hailing from Glasgow, was stationed in North Wales then Germany during his National Service years:

 Some of the National Servicemen had never been away from their homes before, except maybe to the seaside, let alone abroad. I remember in Germany there were two lads who never left the camp, all the time they were there. They spent their spare time in the NAFFI and the canteen, that was it. Apart from an RAF bus transferring them to another camp at one stage, they never saw a square inch of Germany.

When I was stationed in Hawarden, North Wales, there was one bloke who came from nearby so took his washing home to Mum at weekends.

YOUR COUNTRY NEEDS WHO...?

Since 1948 it had been compulsory for all young men to spend the last couple of years of their teens in the Army, and the last 'call up' took place in the mid Fifties. It's still quoted these days by the more right-wing of our elder citizens as *the* answer to all our problems, the perfect way of keeping troublesome teenagers off the streets.

Spotty young boys were packed off to the barracks with their heads shaved, big shiny boots plonked on their feet and evil smelling kitbags slung over their shoulders, and were expected to emerge as model citizens. Most eighteen-year-olds found the Army desperately dull, with long months of boredom spent marooned in the more unpleasant parts of Kenya or Malaya. Certainly two years being screamed at by purple-faced sergeant majors was a serious interruption in a young man's relationship with his mates back home, and many boys came home to find ex-girlfriends married with a couple of kids.

Few former Teds came out of the Army to go back to their DAs and beetle crushers. Young squaddies tended to stick together in pubs and at dances, and when they left the service slipped quietly into adult society.

It was the one thing that helped keep youth rebellion in check in the first half of the Fifties, and its abolition was a turning point for the British teenager.

'RING RING GOES THE BELL'

Virtually every teenager in the land had a target for rebellion in school uniform, which was almost universal in the Fifties. Creativity knew no bounds in efforts to modify bleak blazers and grim gymslips into something approaching cool rather than school, as skirts and heels were subtly raised an inch or two, and ties worn the wrong way round in desperate imitation of the Teds' 'slim jim'.

Many a pubescent Presley was sent home to change out of his blue suede shoes, while even the Royal Navy camel duffel coat was deemed out of order (so immediately adopted by students as a kind of demo uniform the moment they got to college).

Stan Blackman recalls the macho mentality of the Forces:

 Most of the leisure time seemed to be spent drinking and scrapping with the locals. I don't know about helping lads 'grow up' - they went in almost from school, and when they came out they were expected to get married and find a real job - I know it made old men of some of them.

21

'SPLISH SPLASH, I WAS TAKIN' A BATH....'
Teenagers in the Fifties may have been great gangling spotty things - just like today really - but at least the boys smelt nice, and not before time. Until then aftershave and deodorant were anathema to the growing male.

Girls had always been sweet-smelling creatures but the very idea of smelling at least tolerably had always been unthinkable to young men of the Western world. The realisation that people actually preferred having you around, particularly at close quarters, if you didn't smell like a donkey, was a real breakthrough for teenage boys, and quite a bonus for the nostrils of the rest of the population.

But no sooner had demented Dads got used to the idea that their son wearing aftershave didn't signal the onset of transvestitism, then up sprang the Beatniks who decided not to wash at all!

Smell as good as you look with the morning-fresh miracle of bodymist deodorant, aftershave, bathsalts, striped toothpaste (with Chlorophyl!), and the revolutionary all-new triple-head rotary-action Philips Philishave.

BEWARE THE BEATNIK HORROR

In terms of fashion, the Beatniks had all the elegance of the average dustbin, but theirs was a rebellion in lifestyle not just appearance. The black sweaters, black jeans, black stockings, black duffel coats and (preferably) Juliette Greco-inspired long black hair were in no way considered a uniform, but a rejection of any conformity, teenage or otherwise. While most of Fifties youth subscribed to the long-term conventions of go to school, get a job, get married, have kids, retire to Clacton, the British offshoot of the American Beat Generation was having nothing of this.

As kids we knew every word of Kerouac by heart, better than we knew the Bible; although I later realised that most of Jack's writings were the ramblings of an incontinent evil smelling old dosser, at the time he was the author whose book *On The Road* you just had to have poking out of your pocket as you sat for hour after hour in front of a long-gone-cold Cappuccino in the coffee bar.

Although given to studiously avoiding work (a significantly high proportion ended up in Art School), hanging around coffee bars, reading poetry and dabbling in Zen Buddhism, the British Beats were highly motivated when it came to hitchhiking to parties anywhere in the country; in fact hitching, inspired by the Kerouac odyssey, became part of the way of life.

But at least in one direction they were rebels with a cause, the Campaign for Nuclear Disarmament.

BAN, BAN, BAN THE BOMB

Just a dozen years after Hiroshima, as things grew more and more cold between East and West, there was an increasing fear that sooner or later Man would destroy his own planet.

Still at school, Mike Evans recognises he was literally a 'weekend Beatnik':

> ..the Beat writers like Kerouac and Ginsberg were essential reading. I received my first copy of William Burroughs' still-banned Naked Lunch in a brown paper cover, smuggled from a Paris bookshop by a rather hip Liverpool policeman. We would hitch to the nearby bohemia of Liverpool every weekend to listen to jazz, go to poetry readings, watch arty French movies, even smoke some 'charge'...rebellion indeed. And when I thumbed it to Paris to seek out the 'Beat Hotel' where Ginsberg and co apparently hung out, my folks decided I'd gone completely over the top.

even tho it was real stream of consciousness stuff with very little punctuation and dubious speling kerouacs books were like far out man if you dug these literals you were in a solid groove

Paul Harrison (who eventually became a headmaster) grew up in Flintshire, now Clwyd:

> My mother literally broke down in tears when I told her that I not only didn't believe in God, but advocated free love as well; I don't know which upset her most.

23

John Banks from Bolton went on the first CND march from Trafalgar Square to the Atomic Weapons Research Establishment at Aldermaston in 1958:

Coming from a solid Labour background - my father's favourite saying was 'They'll change nothing till they nationalise the banks' - meant that to revolt against family (which was crucial) one had to be either highly reactionary or revolutionary. Joining CND was, for them, beyond the pale, and when I hitchhiked to London for the march, I may as well have been leaving for Mars. They thought I'd flipped.

'Beatnik girls? - half a page of Bertrand Russell and they're putty in your hands' - well that's what Tony Hancock said on his hit show 'Hancock's Half Hour'.

CND had huge support in the late Fifties, and as a kid growing up in Berkshire the long lines of marchers trudging from Aldermaston to London were a familiar annual sight. Although many of its leaders were elder statesmen, it attracted rebellious youngsters like flies. For perhaps the very first time the young people of Britain were making a statement against the real mess that their parents had made of things. It was also of course a damn good weekend; you slept rough, met a lot of girls and there were plenty of pubs at the nightly stop-overs. Though quite how you were supposed to get girls into trouble while walking non-stop to London I never did find out. There was rarely any trouble, and even the frustrated motorists crawling along the A4 took it all in good part. But in spite of its lofty intentions, most parents were violently opposed to it, seeing it as a hotbed of vice, promiscuity and political subversion.

FROTHING AT THE MOUTH

It wasn't just the Beatnik fraternity that patronised the coffee bars of course - if it had been, the espresso emporiums would have gone broke within a matter of weeks. A reaction to post-war ration book austerity - food was still subject to your quota of 'points' until 1953 - they were the first pioneers in the fast-food revolution to come. But more importantly for teenagers, they quickly became a haunt they could call their own. Pubs were still considered strictly adult in the early and middle Fifties, and run on strictly traditional lines - certainly no jukeboxes, which is where the new Formica-clad coffee bars came in as an adolescent attraction.

The craze for frothy coffee accompanied by music mushroomed around the middle of the decade - for once not an American import but from Italy where lounging around all day chatting up chicks was a national sport. Very

Coffee bar style: smooth surfaces and contemporary legs - the furniture looked modern too!

Tea......4d. Coffee......6d
Customers are requested to vacate their seats after a
reasonable time to allow other patrons to sit down.
No lounging...No loitering...No bad language.

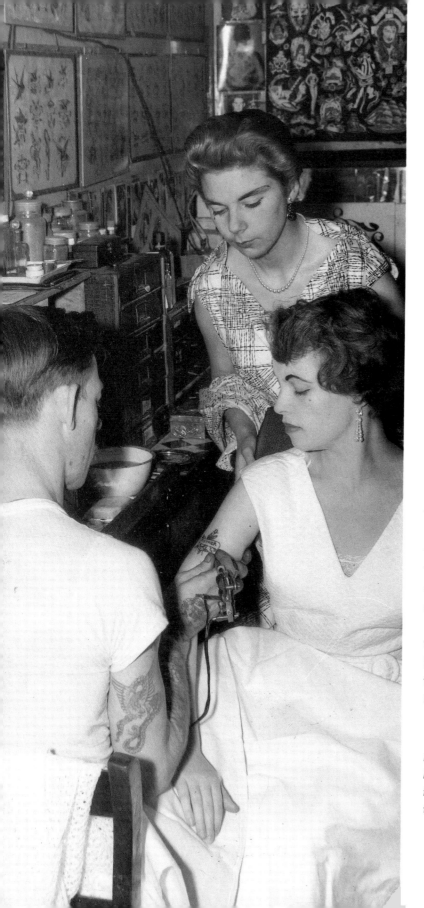

soon 'theme' coffee houses catered for all teenage tastes; there were the regular rock'n'roll places - in fact many of the first British rock stars like Tommy Steele and Marty Wilde were launched from London's '2 Is'- as well as those featuring folk music, skiffle, jazz, to the more esoteric 'left-wing' establishments like the Partisan in Soho where the po-faced punters preferred chess and poetry - very renegade.

The importance of the jukebox in most coffee bars can't be overestimated; at a time when radio still catered largely for the Mum-and-Dad generation, it was crucial in the popularity of rock'n'roll, away from parental nagging when you played your latest Elvis disc at top volume. The other main venues for the voluminous jukebox - huge exotic Wurlitzers playing 78s for a threepenny bit were still the norm in 1956, the high-tech Bal Ami and Rock-Ola 45 machines appearing soon after - were fairgrounds and amusement arcades.

Apart from travelling fairs which visited towns a couple of times a year, they were to be found on a permanent basis in seaside resorts. From the mid Fifties onwards they became a focal point for miscreant youth; girls who hung round fairgrounds were considered 'loose', boys 'up to no good'. You could even visit a seedy tattoo artist for the permanent brand of rebellion to be inscribed forever, sending parents into paroxisms of despair. They were an automatic magnet to teenagers.

With their fast rides, fast music and (supposedly) fast women, fairgrounds played host to hordes of leather-clad bikers who continued to make the pilgrimage en masse through the mods-and-rockers confrontations of the Sixties till today.

My Mum was always saying to me 'You've got to be different, haven't you..?' as if there was something wrong in that. The final straw was when I got tatooed - she went bananas, even though it was a heart with 'MUM & DAD' inscribed in it.

Even more dubious from society's point of view were the characters who worked the fairs. As well as the seasonal summer workers, a motley bunch of out of work actors, students on vacation and the otherwise unemployable, there was a whole subculture of dropped-out teenagers who worked the fairs on a full-time basis - often runaways from home - who avoided all normal contact with 'regular' society, be it teacher or taxman.

THE PRINCE OF WAILS

The major factor that distanced the previous generation from coffee bars, fairgrounds and such was the music. Music, and particularly rock'n'roll, was the cultural identity around which teenage attitudes - and rebellion - revolved.

The Fifties was a great musical watershed. It all started in 1950-51 with Johnnie Ray who was a one-man watershed in his own right. His huge hit 'Cry' had everyone reduced to tears, and his onstage gimmick was to break down sobbing as he delivered 'Cry', 'The Little White Cloud That Cried' and other world-shaking weepies. Variously known as the 'Cry Guy', 'Nabob of Sob' and

'Prince of Wails', Ray brought spontaneous histrionics to song delivery for the first time, heralding the gyrations of Elvis a little later in the decade. He was an habitual blubberer, a cry baby, by any normal macho standards a total wimp, but his performances did wonders for handkerchief sales and produced a genuine hysteria in his teenage (mainly female) audience. which was then quite unique.

Summer holidays, you worked the fairgrounds for three reasons - the birds, the fiddle and the wages, in that order.

In 1952 Wendy Woodhouse went on her first holiday away from her parents, with three girlfriends to Butlins in Filey:

We were told there were 8,000 boys to 4,000 girls. At night we jostled for room in the small chalet to make ourselves glamorous in our party frocks and big flowery earrings. At night the camp seemed even more glamorous, lit by coloured lights. We couldn't wait, first a show by the Red Coats, then dancing in the big ballroom to the Joe Daniels Band.

They may have only been two-dimensional heroes, but what more could a girl ask for, be it a moody Marty, lip-curling Cliff or paper Presley. Hardly Dad's idea of DIY wallpaper though.

Johnnie Ray-vers were often ready to rip the sobbing singer to shreds, while Haley hooligans just settled for the seats.

Far from them shouting things like 'For God's sake John, control yourself', he touched a deep emotion in the young pubescent army of females that followed him. And alongside the sobs and howls a new sound could be heard. Quite unmistakable from the mouths of the adoring bobby-soxers, it was a squeal. To be more specific it was a high-pitched noise of sexual ecstasy, triggered by something as arousing as 'Hallo there', which carried on through all the songs until the nice man said 'Bye Bye'.

And to top it all, some of Johnnie's records were banned by the then all-powerful BBC. As the Rolling Stones, the Sex Pistols, Frankie Goes To Hollywood and others were to learn later, there's nothing like being banned to sell records; it becomes an act of rebellion just to go out and buy them, and it was even more so in 1951.

ROCK'N'ROLL MADNESS

Rock'n'roll really arrived in 1954 with Bill Haley and the Comets; Haley was already going on thirty, a greasy oil slick of a man with terminal acne, a face like a bag of chisels and a curious taste in suits, but the raw driving beat of the new music was to take over the world.

On 12th April 1954 Bill and his merry men popped into a recording studio for about twenty minutes, bashed out fairly harmless versions of two R&B tunes, 'Shake Rattle and Roll' and 'Rock Around The Clock', and a whole new musical era began - and one which had teenage rebellion stamped all over it right from the start.

Sandra Burton was there when Bill Haley made his dynamic debut:

When Bill Haley arrived in England in February 1957, there was a special train organised by the Daily Mirror to meet him at Southampton. I won a ticket and we left Waterloo station, jiving to rock'n'roll records all the way there.

Bill and The Comets came back on the train and we were all met by thousands more fans at Waterloo. It was almost a riot, the police and railway people didn't know what had hit them. When my parents saw all the screaming teenagers on the Movietone News at the local cinema the following week, they went mad. You would think I'd been involved in some kind of orgy, they didn't let me out (except for school) for a fortnight.

'Rock Around The Clock' was part of the soundtrack of the MGM film 'The Blackboard Jungle', and the scenes that greeted the movie in Britain were like nothing before. The film was no masterpiece, and about as much fun as Christmas Day 'Bullseye', but it was about the fast-spreading notion that teenagers were revolting. When the Haley tune heralded the opening scene audiences erupted. It was the signal for dancing in the aisles, acrobatic jiving at that, for which you needed a bit of room.... and the only way to make room was to rip the seats out. Cinema managers could be seen all over the UK in the days long before pocket calculators, trying to work out the profit and loss balance between massive ticket sales and replacement furniture.

Beaming Bill Haley. The Kiss-Curled One was - albeit briefly - the undisputed King of Rock'n'Roll..........until his crown was well and truly stolen by the pulsating pelvis of Elvis, parading the parts the TV cameras couldn't reach.

'My vines are all green, my potatoes red,
I thought you was my friend till I caught you in my bed'
- lurid lyrics that got Lonnie Donegan's 'Digging My Potatoes'
banned by the ever-vigilant BBC.

Nice clean men in shiny suits still dominated the music market of course, Frankie Laine, Guy Mitchell, David Whitfield and the rest appealing to an 'across the board' audience - which made the next stage in the rock revolution even more potent, the arrival of Elvis Presley.

Already a legend for his sexual gyrations that had him banned from American TV from the waist down, Elvis with his explicitly sensual records and moody Brandoish looks was the ultimate icon for teen rebellion. For parents he was everything they didn't want their sons to be or their daughters to meet, for their teenage offspring just the opposite.

In Britain we had the young Cliff, who looks marginally younger today over thirty years later, only with much nicer teeth. Other emerging British heart-throbs were Tommy Steele, Adam Faith and Marty Wilde.

IT'S NOT ONLY ROCK'N'ROLL

The other great musical milestone of Fifties teenage Britain was skiffle. Launched by Lonnie Donegan, who perfected a technique of singing through his nose while miming with his mouth, it provided a do-it-yourself form of music based on American folksongs and blues which had thousands of youthful skifflers strumming guitars, and thumping home-made tea chest basses and washboards. Front-parlour rehearsals were guaranteed to annoy parents even more than the records they objected to so much.

Jazz, although more of a minority craze - today it would be called a cult music - was equally despised by parents. Whether 'trad' or 'modern', it was deemed tuneless and cacophonous, with sinister connotations associated with the dark cellar jazz clubs that were opening everywhere, from drug taking to uninhibited sex. And not only did our parents hate the sound, the volume and the content of the new records, they couldn't break the damn things either. A major development in a decade of technological marvels was the plastic vinyl record. Until then all records had been 10" shellac 78s which were easily shattered. Many an illicit teenage get-together while parents were out was ruined by a careless botty sitting on a pile of 78s that had been left with equal carelessness on the sofa. To my own eternal shame I once sat on Elvis' 'All Shook Up' and 'Heartbreak Hotel' in a single wet Saturday afternoon. I had to shell out nearly three shillings to replace them out of my pocket money before anybody would speak to me again. Today, they'd probably each fetch hundreds of pounds.

The other great mechanical breakthrough was the now-legendary Dansette Major. This record player was probably in more teenagers' bedrooms in the late Fifties than any other single item. The great bonus of the Dansette Major was that it could play the vinyl 45s, EPs and LPs - and more than one at a time. A whole pile of two-minute singles could be piled up one on top of the other and played non-stop for half an hour.....all the more to annoy the folks with, not to mention less interruptions to necking sessions at parties.

It was also the era of the first really portable radio, the transistor set or 'tranny' which could be taken anywhere...the Walkman of its day, turned up loud it was far more anti-social and another device to bug grown-ups.

Judy Ford from Macclesfield remembers the furore well:

My first real pop record was Lonnie Donegan's 'Rock Island Line' which my father forbade me to play on his gramophone. He considered modern music would be the downfall of civilisation.

Andy Driver caught the skiffle bug when it swept the country:

Jazz was our religion, skiffle and blues its do-it-yourself songbook. The songs were about railroad men, escaped convicts, murdered lovers - none of your moon-in-June stuff.

The latest in lurex-luxury listening - pastel colour coordinated in beautiful mock nylon with an elegant plastic trim.

I WAS A TEENAGE PETE MURRAY

For rock'n'roll, radio gradually came into its own as the natural medium. Everyone had been brought up on the 'wireless' of course, but the obligatory Sunday lunchtime 'Family Favourites' and 'Billy Cotton Bandshow' when pop hits were sandwiched between light classics and music hall melodies were anathema to teenagers.

Rebellion on radio found its expression in the programmes parents didn't want to hear or, better still, didn't even understand. The audio anarchy of the Goons was a case in point, where the surreal mayhem of Spike Milligan, Peter Sellers and Harry Secombe captivated a juvenile generation while parents stood back simply nonplussed.

Even more subversive, shows devoted entirely to rock'n'roll records were broadcast from Radio Luxembourg to be picked up, often under clandestine bedclothes late at night, on the new 'tranny'.

Television was likewise aimed at a 'family audience' in its battle for the attention of a populace that still attended the cinema twice a week in the mid Fifties.

I remember spending hours of my formative prepubescent years standing on a stool in front of the telly trying to peep down the front of a lady called Sylvia Peters' dresses. No

'Big Brother Is Watching You' was a Fifties catch-phrase after a TV version of '1984' caused an overnight sensation....while the Box spread to every home in the land.

matter how high up I stood I didn't seem able to see any further down her cleavage. I couldn't understand it then, and I don't really understand it today, although I have more or less stopped doing it, except when Judith Chalmers comes on. Nevertheless, alongside the quiz shows like 'Take Your Pick' and 'Double Your Money' and American sit-coms typified by 'I Love Lucy' and 'I Married Joan' there were genuine attempts to appeal to the new teen market - being on national prime-time TV they were hardly representative of teen rebellion, but managed to hint at it from time to time. Of the best remembered, the BBC's 'Six-Five Special' was rather like a local church youth club, with a young-ish Pete Murray taking the place of the genial with-it vicar, but it did feature live rock'n'roll, skiffle and jazz, and was enough to send parents scurrying from the room.

ITV's 'Oh Boy' was altogether more frenetic, with the cream of British rockers - Billy Fury, Marty Wilde, Adam Faith, Cuddly Duddly et al - banging out a non-stop sequence of hits in front of a live and screaming audience of genuine fans.

The shows lacked a lot of the technical wizardry of today's televised pop, and the sound of the artists was often inaudible over the squeals of the girl fans, but they were a tremendous live event and have rarely been bettered. Most important of all, Mums and Dads absolutely hated them.

More obscure pop programmes included two that appeared soon after the debut of commercial television in 1955 which were even more bizarrely teen-oriented in their own way, the manic Sunday night 'Jack Jackson Show' and 'Cool For Cats' introduced by wrestling-commentator-to-be Kent Walton; both shows featured miming to records rather than live performance, and often the miming was done by the regular cast of dancers/comedians rather than the actual artists!

'It's time to jive on the old Six-Five' was the welcome from post-teenage presenters Pete Murray and Josephine Douglas, and resident raver Don Lang with his Frantic Five.

Parental wrath over radio rock could be ferocious, as Paul Goldsby relates from his schooldays in Lincolnshire:

My Mum used to come and switch my bedroom light off after eleven-thirty, but 'Luxy' went on till two so I'd have the radio under the bedclothes. If she caught me, she just took the radio away. There was one kid in our class whose Dad was a religious fanatic of some kind, and whipped him with a leather belt then made him learn a chapter of the Bible by heart, just for listening to Elvis records on Luxembourg!

'The slippery slope to hellfire and damnation is lined with neon-lit temptations that the teenagers of today find hard to resist' - The Reverend Thomas Jones-Williams, The Daily Post (North Wales edition) June 1958.

DIG THIS

ROCK around the
clock

Brunswick
RECORDS

ROCK

ROCK AROUND THE CLOCK   MAMBO ROCK
SEE YOU LATER, ALLIGATOR   R-O-C-K

BILL HALEY AND HIS COMETS

Fantabulous
Player
by EMI

Film censorship presented its problems for Jim McEwan of Glasgow:

> *In my early teens we used to have to ask an adult to 'take us in' to an 'A' picture, and if it was an 'X' - more usually horror than sex in those days - then out of desperation we'd 'bunk in' the back exit. The sex films that did cause a stir, we never stopped talking about them in school, were Carrol Baker in 'Baby Doll' or anything with Brigitte Bardot.*

SITTIN' IN THE BACK ROW

While 'the telly' established itself as an increasingly important part of our fast changing world in the Fifties, the cinema continued to play an important part in our leisure time. Although it had been the main medium for previous generations going back to the Twenties, it was still crucial to teenagers as one of the few places you could get away from Mum and Dad, especially for the privacy of a date. The back row at Reading Gaumont when the lights went down was full of slobbering couples licking each other like postage stamps.

The cinema may have been the place to take your new girlfriend for the chance of a bit of 'thigh top', but it was also where one paid homage to the new teen heroes of the silver screen.

It was the time when to mumble was to be magnificent. 'On The Waterfront' starred the slender, muscular young Marlon Brando, a figure looking less like the obese slobbering Brando of the Nineties than anything on this planet. And judging by his brief but crazed appearance on earth, 'Rebel Without A Cause' James Dean might well have looked equally raddled had he reached Brando's age; but he died at the age of 23, driving much too fast, and by dying young was guaranteed a fame and cult status among teenagers of the day that he might never otherwise have achieved.....he was simply the teenager-as-rebel-without-a-cause personified. In fact, had he lived, by now he could have been rebel without a clue.

In fact the ads for 'Rebel' said it all, under a picture of Dean and co-star Natalie Wood - 'the bad boy from a "good" family'.

Female pin-ups proliferated as well of course. While Marilyn Monroe appealed to males of all ages, the last of the great Hollywood glamour goddesses, inspiring the lurid imagination of spotty youths across the Western world in a series of steamy subtitled sagas was the ultimate kohl-eyed 'sex kitten' Brigitte Bardot.

Idol worship took on a macabre slant with the James Dean cult, as Carol Wilson remembers:

I was a 'Dean-ager' - that's what we James Dean fans called ourselves. He was already dead by the time his first film 'East Of Eden' was released, so my Mum and Dad thought I was a little peculiar having his photographs all over my bedroom - even one of his car crash. I went to see 'Rebel Without A Cause' every night for a week when it was on at our local picture house.

A Savage Story of lust and ambition

SIMONE SIGNORET
LAURENCE HARVEY
HEATHER SEARS

THE FILM OF
JOHN BRAINE'S
Scorching
BESTSELLER

ROOM AT THE TOP

co-starring
DONALD WOLFIT
DONALD HOUSTON
HERMIONE BADDELEY

BRYANSTON PRESENTS—A WOODFALL PRODUCTION

ALBERT FINNEY   SHIRLEY ANNE FIELD

SATURDAY NIGHT and SUNDAY MORNING

RACHEL ROBERTS

FROM THE NOVEL BY ALAN SILLITOE · PRODUCED BY HARRY SALTZMAN & TONY RICHARDSON
DIRECTED BY KAREL REISZ · SCREENPLAY BY ALAN SILLITOE
DISTRIBUTED BY BRITISH LION FILMS IN ASSOCIATION WITH BRYANSTON FILMS

Films like 'Saturday Night And Sunday Morning' at the end of the decade featured local beer-and-chips anti-heroes that we all identified with.

The back row of the Odeon, Rhyl, looms large in Mike Evans' memory:

> *The first night a girl put her hand inside my trousers was during a Kenneth Moore film about the sinking of the Titanic. It was called 'A Night To Remember'.*

C.A. Garrett, from Bristol, remembers the movie debut of Elvis:

> *We screamed, we rocked, and when his first film came to Bristol it was if every teenager in the town had descended on the cinema; the queue stretched for miles. As soon as he appeared on the screen everyone left their seats and screamed so loudly not a word he said could be heard. The manager tried to restore order but it was impossible.*

The Fifties re-established the days of the Great Movie Star after the hiccup of the war years. Charlton Heston almost died driving his chariot in the epic 'Ben Hur', and Laurence Olivier created the definitive Richard the Third; established names like Gregory Peck, Burt Lancaster, and Kirk Douglas continued to make girls go all gooey and unnecessary, and Rock Hudson was voted Dishiest Man On Earth by one US girlie magazine.

But it was the new kind of star that excited teenagers, and a new kind of movie.

As well as Dean and Brando, a whole group of actors sharing the 'Method' style revolutionised on-screen realism, including Montgomery Clift, Anthony Perkins, Carrol Baker, and Paul Newman. In Britain too, films by the best-selling 'angry young men' writers - 'Look Back In Anger', 'Room At The Top '- were box office smashes. And, for the first time, it was the era of the teen movie - apart from Dean's 'Rebel' and Brando's 'Wild One', these were usually low-budget 'exploitation' pics with lurid titles ranging from 'High School Hellcats' and 'Juvenile Jungle' to the now-legendary 'I Was A Teenage Werewolf'.

Mamie Van Doren with her hour-glass figure and seductive poses, was the queen of the teen B-movie, starring in dozens of adolescent epics like 'The Young Hellions', 'Running Wild', 'College Confidential', 'The Beat Generation' and 'Untamed Youth' which had teenagers queueing round the block, and parents merely glad they'd invested £60 in their 12" black-and-white TV.

Plus of course there were the rock'n'roll films. The first was Bill Haley's 'Rock Around The Clock', which despite a pathetic plot and wooden acting - ending with the middle-aged 'hep cats' clicking their fingers out of time to the jolly rock'n'roll they'd initially condemned - resulted in as much seat-slashing and general mayhem

Margaret Barker of Cheshire was mad about dancing, maybe three or four times a week:

Monday was 2/6d night if you could beg an extra 2/6d from parents. These were the days we handed our wages over to Mum who gave us back 'spends' which often only lasted till Monday. Friday was 'Big Band Night' and tickets only. We saw many visiting bands - Johnny Dankworth with the very young and beautiful Cleo Laine, Ted Heath, Ray Ellington with the bosomy Marion Ryan, Eric Delaney - a manic drummer - and Chris Barber's Jazz Band.

In the interval at the Palais de Danse we grabbed a 'pass-out' and sneaked into the corner pub hoping we would look old enough to order a gin and orange, and if we were lucky to get a boy to take us in and pay for it.

Burton the Tailors had a billiard saloon above many of their branches, and a small dance hall above that - the source of a rather juvenile dirty joke involving trouser fitting, snooker and the ballroom.

as had 'Blackboard Jungle' a few months before. This was followed by the first moving glimpse of Elvis for British teenagers in his mainly-acting role in 'Love Me Tender', and an avalanche of cheapo pop pics like 'Disc Jockey Jamboree' and 'Rock, Rock, Rock' which were merely strung together cameos of what now would be promo videos of rockstars.

AT THE HOP

Apart from the 'pictures' the other social high-spot was the (usually) Saturday night dance. Held in local youth clubs or church halls as often as in proper dancehalls, they were strange ritualistic affairs where the girls sat all along the wall and the boys spent most of the evening trying to pretend they didn't even know the soppy things were there, until the last couple of dances when there was a mad stampede to try and get 'fixed up' before all the lights came back on again and the band started to pack up to go home to their beds.

The actual dancing was a strange mixture of styles in the Fifties. It was a decade that began with the Jitterbug and ended with the first hints of the Twist. The first teen breakthrough was the bizarre Creep, which was mercifully short lived, basically because you looked like a pair of freshly neutered ferrets as you shuffled across the dancefloor, and was about as much fun as hitting yourself over the head with a three-week-old dogfish.

The big one of course was the Jive.

An adaptation of Jitterbug, it was part and parcel of rock'n'roll and Teddy Boys and Girls made a real meal of the whole thing, the boys throwing their squealing beehived partners over their shoulders and between their drainpiped legs. It was also adopted by the growing army of trad jazz fans, in their long chunky jumpers and oh-so-daring sandals. Their duffel coats of course were left hanging in a neat line in the cloakroom.

Jim was already fixing it for a lot of teenagers like Wendy Woodhouse of Manchester over thirty years ago:

Lunchtime was magic. That was when we went bopping round our handbags at the Plaza, a small ballroom over a restaurant, for sixpence....the DJ was Jimmy Savile, even then a way-out character with dyed hair and a leopard skin suit.

The great invention of the Fifties was a dance for people who didn't have a partner, or were too drunk to get to their feet anyway, and that was the Hand Jive. I remember enviously watching a line of Hand Jivers sitting in a coffee bar all waving their little arms like dervishes to Gene Vincent on the jukebox. It looked like fabulous fun at the time, but on reflection was about as enjoyable as an attack of the mumps.

What made the Hand Jive irresistible was that our parents were convinced we'd finally flipped. Unfortunately our Mums and Dads gradually discovered its attractions, and it was then we abandoned it in disgust. It's sadly missed, as it remains one of the very few dances I ever really mastered. Indeed the Hand Jive, Headbanging and the Pogo remain more or less my full range to this day, those and a sort of drunken grope.

HALFWAY TO PARADISE

Essential to youth rebellion was the breaking of taboos. Cigarette smoking, though not considered a health hazard in those days, was still a cloak-and-dagger affair in one's early teens, though everyone was puffing away by the time they first ventured into a pub for an illicit half of mild beer months before their eighteenth birthday. Pubs were still the domain of adults, hence the coffee bar culture which persisted into the Sixties, so drinking tended to involve bottles of cheap wine or cider at suburban parties - preferably when someones parents were safely away for the weekend.

But the big taboo was sex.

Apart from the picture house and the darker corners of a dancehall, there were very few places for 'courting couples' to be alone. Few teenagers had the use of the back seat of Dad's Austin 7, and it was often the choice

P. Hefford of Derby, who now lives in Rochester, Kent, attended dances at her local church youth club:

Boys and girls were separated between locked doors. The boys played billiards, while the girls learned to knit or sew. Then at nine o'clock the door was unlocked and we merged to dance to the gramophone. Nat King Cole was a great favourite, and we smooched to 'Ramblin Rose' and 'Walkin' My Baby Back Home'. At ten we paired off, kissed in the churchyard and hurried home.

Mother allowed ten minutes for the journey and then she was standing on the doorstep waiting for me. The punishment for being late was plain and simple - a week without youth club.

Kids! Be the first in your youth club to learn to jive the easy way! Just send 2/- inc. post and packing for Victor Sylvester's step-by-step course.

Mr and Mrs Mycock from Middleton, Manchester, had to go to court to get permission to wed:

I left school when I was sixteen and fell madly in love with a man of twenty. My parents were devastated and forbid me to see him again, but I loved him so much I left home. My father sent the police to fetch me back, but because I had a place to stay and a job there was nothing they could do. After a few weeks Trevor and I wanted to marry and needed my Dad to give his permission because I was so young. He refused so we sought permission from the court. I was made a ward of court which caused such a scandal, and a few weeks later the judge sent for us and gave us his permission to marry. We didn't see my parents until two years later when they finally forgave us. We've now been married for thirty-two years.

of a bus shelter or a park after dark. Most teenagers still lived at home - hence the liberating effect on students when they went to college - and this caused the inevitable problems of groping in the front room with Mum in the next room watching the telly.

Hardly any teenagers had cars of their own, so the last tram or bus was the only way to get girls home, often for a furtive necking session on the doorstep before a long walk home for the rampant young male.

Sexual activity was usually rather a limited affair. Very few girls would go 'all the way' before marriage; contraception was limited to the ubiquitous 'packet of three' which few girls trusted the boys to use properly, with good reason. Three and ninepence for just three Durex was a lot of money, and a lot of less than scrupulous youths were known to use the same 'johnny' several times, with several girls, over several weeks. The girlfriend couldn't then understand why, having taken precautions, she found herself 'in the family way', and the boyfriend had disappeared without trace to do National Service at a barracks 'somewhere near Berlin'. The contraceptive pill had been developed in 1955 but wasn't mass produced until the Sixties, so sex in the Fifties was mainly a case of grubby little boys trying to see how far disappointingly wholesome girls would 'go' before they got a slap in the face. It was usually at the point where the boy's pudgy sweating little hands finally touched the smooth area of skin above the girl's stocking tops. At this point there was a sharp crack across the boy's cheek, followed by a lot of hurried buttoning up noises and sobbed recriminations about not being 'that sort of girl'.

'Dirty' magazines included 'Spick and Span', 'Razzle', and the naturist 'Health and Efficiency'; caught with any of them and you were in deep trouble. Not to mention the cheap paperback thrillers by Hank Jansen - steamy stuff!

Sadly for the teenage boys of the early rock'n'roll years, there weren't many of 'that sort of girl' about at all, so they just had to suffer the constant face slappings and live in hope.

FROM RATIONING TO ROCKING

Although the Fifties seem less clearly defined, less charismatic and colourful than the decades that were to follow, they were certainly the fastest moving years, the ones that saw the most real changes.

It was when teen rebellion first shocked the adult world of the squares, a world that was in a state of flux as never before.........

The end of food rationing. War in Korea. Sightings of flying saucers. The first space satellites. The last death penalty. Burgess and Maclean. Lord and Lady Docker. The Suez crisis. The Hungarian revolution. The death of Stalin. The conquest of Everest. Castro and Guevara taking Cuba. The Cold War. The Bomb.

And of course coffee bars, swooning bobby soxers, blue suede shoes, The Big Bopper, the Blackboard Jungle, skiffle, 'Look Back In Anger', 'Room At The Top', beehive hairdos, Elvis, the end of the call-up, Cool For Cats, jazz clubs, handjiving, and all the other beginnings of the youth revolution.

Jive contests and dance marathons were one way of sorting out the swinging cats from the squares. On the other hand a real cool chick just closed her eyes and dug those crazy sounds.

60s

BORN TO BE WILD

Joey Pumford of Newport, Gwent, remembers the traumas of the first 'grown up' dance he went to:

I shouldn't have been there really as I wasn't quite fifteen and the dance was supposedly for adults. But there I was, all togged up in my first long-trousered suit and my fancy silk shirt, feeling quite happy as I'd had two pints of bitter when all of a sudden a vision of loveliness came up to me and said 'Hello'. I was a bit nervous at first as the girl was all of sixteen but I soon calmed down and asked her for a dance. Her green eyes sparkled as I held her close. The band went up tempo and we danced faster. We were really enjoying ourselves as we jigged and shook, faster and faster, and closer and closer. Then suddenly, crunch! my head collided with the girl's nose. She screamed then passed out cold, blood streaming from her pretty nose which I thought I'd broken. The bouncers came over and I ran away terrified. A good job as they were her brothers. They were very angry, and rumour had it that I was about to lose an arm or a leg, or worse. It took months of diplomacy before I was able to return.

I remember the opening seconds of the Sixties. It was the first time my parents had let me stay up till midnight, and in a little house in Reading we all wished each other Happy New Decade to the grating bagpipes of a Scottish marching band on something quite dreadful called the White Heather Club on our little black and white telly. I don't think I felt particularly swinging at any time through the next ten years, and to be truthful I don't think ninety percent of the population knew they were really part of the Swinging Sixties either until some time round the mid Seventies when social historians told us in graphic detail about all the fun we'd missed.

In fact, in many ways after all the promise of the rock'n'roll years of the late Fifties, the dawn of the new decade was all a bit of a let down.

It almost seemed as if the youth rebellion of the last few years was over, or at least taking a bit of a breather.

BYE BYE, JOHNNY B. GOODE

In 1960 the quite revoltingly squeaky clean Frankie Avalon (along with others of his ilk) was the number one heart throb, and hardly any of the first wave of rock heroes were still rocking.

Elvis had gone wholesome and become an all round entertainer of all things and had more or less stopped the writhing sexual pelvic contortions that had just about got him excommunicated in his Hound Dog years, and was making quite dreadful records like 'It's Now or Never' and 'Are You Lonesome Tonight?'.

I don't think he was particularly lonesome any night, but he certainly deserved to be. The King of Rock'n'Roll also had a nasty habit of turning up on American TV shows, backslapping, grinning and guffawing with people like the 'Pack', Dean Martin, Peter Lawford and other heroes of establishment USA, and Hot Hips of only three years before had become part of something altogether more Ivy League.

We all felt terribly let down. In addition he was beginning to release a whole string of quite the worst films in the history of the world. I remember sleeping soundly through every second of 'Kid Galahad' in Reading Gaumont, and a few months later there was a merciful power cut after only about the first ten minutes of 'Clambake'... none of us even pestered the manager to try and get the projector working again, and I don't even think we asked for our money back. We were just glad to get away from the whole dreadful business.

But at least Elvis was still alive, some say he still is, running a hamburger joint in Chicago, but Buddy Holly was dead, Eddie Cochran was killed early in April 1960, Gene Vincent badly injured in the same car crash, and Chuck Berry and Jerry Lee Lewis were more or less banned from appearing anywhere in the world ever again for being too smutty - in their lifestyles as well as music - for the still conservative taste of the moral majority.

Bob Reed felt the pressure to conform:

You went out with a girl for more than a year and you were asked 'When are you getting engaged?'. If you got engaged, next it was 'When are you getting married?'. You got married and it was 'You must get a house and a mortgage!' and 'When are you starting a family?'. It all seemed so boring and ordinary to me. Why should everyone do what their parents did? Looking back, the sad thing is most of us ended up doing just that.

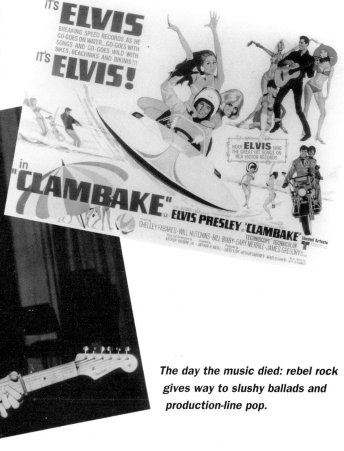

The day the music died: rebel rock gives way to slushy ballads and production-line pop.

The Bomb wasn't the only thing we were anxious to stop at the open air gatherings of the Sixties.

CAN'T GET NO SATISFACTION

Though the rockers had gone, the dissatisfaction remained among the younger generation with the world our parents had created for us, and looked like there was every chance of destroying. CND was as busy as ever in the early Sixties, as the fierce rivalry between the USA and the Soviet Union over everything from nuclear weapons to the Space Race was intensifying; as teenagers we were all sure that the world might very well go bang. Several times in the next few years it very nearly did.

France became the fourth power to have the atomic bomb, the Russians built a wall separating East from West Berlin, and Eisenhower and Khrushchev continued to flex their muscles across the globe with us feeling very much like the little piggy in the middle. I remember a lot of us kids talked about the end of the world, and really felt it was imminent.

We had a school essay to write when I was about fourteen: 'How would you spend your last four minutes on earth, after the four-minute warning of nuclear war?' I seem to remember I wanted to spend mine with Daphne Bolton. When the essays were collected up, I discovered that most of the rest of the class wanted to spend their final moments with Miss Bolton as well, so for Daphne it could have been a hell of a send-off...

Quite what we'd have done with Daphne I don't know.

A lot of kissing with eyes and lips firmly closed I suspect (Michael Aspel once told me on a TV show he still does) because certainly there was no sense yet of any new sexual freedoms.

The Pill arrived in 1961, but was available to 'married couples only' until later, when it was begrudgingly distributed to any couples having a 'solid, meaningful relationship of some long standing'.

We may have advocated 'free love' but things didn't always go according to plan. Joey Pumford's introduction to the female form, for example, albeit in the pages of a book, was a torturous affair:

I walked into the art class at school and saw a bunch of boys gathered at the front of the class. I went to have a look and discovered the boys had found a picture of a nude model. Being only thirteen at the time I was quite unknowledgeable of the female form and stood spellbound, observing the various bumps and curves. So engrossed was I that I failed to notice the art teacher enter the room. 'What're you looking at boy?' he hissed. 'Nothing Sir'. He grabbed me by the ear and marched me out of the classroom down to the headmaster's office. The headmaster beckoned me into his inner sanctum then launched into a diatribe, using large words such as 'masturbation' and 'perversion', words I didn't know the meanings of. What would you expect from a thirteen-year-old who'd never kissed a girl, let alone seen one in the nude.

And for Mrs L. Ridgeway of Peel Green, Manchester, just meeting the opposite sex didn't necessarily spell success:

When I was nineteen, in Summer 1964, I went on holiday to Torquay with my girlfriend. We were young for our age, but willing to try out our wings as far as meeting new men was concerned. My friend was confident on dates and chatted away easily to boys while I was easily tongue-tied. Consequently the next day I was usually stood up, and had to sit there like a gooseberry.

I decided to try to remedy the situation and spent all my money on a very tight, short shift dress. However, my dreams were never realised and I had to sell the dress to my friend for money to spend on the way back to Manchester.

They weren't always too careful of course; I did once manage to convince the fierce lady who held the keys to the Pill cupboard at a well-known Birmingham clinic that I was having a 'solid, meaningful and longstanding' relationship with a girl I'd only met on the bus earlier that morning.

Generally though I have to concede, along with the great majority of teenage males of the Sixties, that there was nothing very swinging about our love lives.

It seemed like the majority of girls were hopping into bed with David Bailey and Mick Jagger, perhaps even at the same time, while the rest of us boys were getting no more than a series of irate face-slaps for trying to 'get past the stocking tops'.

Despite all the hype about promiscuity and the endless 'summers of love' that we heard about in the late Sixties, sixty-three percent of women were still virgins when they married in 1969 and another twenty-six percent had only had sexual experience with the man they eventually married.

According to my calculations this leaves just eleven percent who must have been absolute ravers. So where were they when we needed them? Presumably with Mick Jagger or David Bailey.

'Badges declaring the wearer's politics, sexual preferences and so on, clearly have their roots in the fertility symbols and rituals of primitive man'.

Anthropology discussion, BBC Third Programme

SCANDAL!

But while we waited for something to happen in rock'n'roll, from the start of the decade things were happening in other areas and happening fast. The show trial of the decade was publishers Penguin being taken to court over the publication of D.H. Lawrence's novel *Lady Chatterley's Lover*. The book is a fairly dull tale of the Lady of the Manor's torrid affair with her lusty gamekeeper, though well laced with four-letter words and sexual description. It probably wouldn't have sold more than a few hundred copies if the Director of Public Prosecutions hadn't decided to try and stop it ever getting onto the bookshelves.

Penguin won the day, and it exposed a great gulf between 'them' and 'us' which was typified by the Prosecuting Counsel's remark '...but is it a book you would ever wish your wife or your servants to read?'. It was a gulf which seemed particularly archaic to teenagers, and was to herald a revolution which 'they' were completely unprepared for.

Again on the literary front, the satirical magazine 'Private Eye' made its appearance on the news stands and was eagerly read by young people in particular.

Boys in my boarding school in Worcester were caned just for having it in their posession. It was of some satisfaction when I was caught reading 'Pseud's Corner' under the bedclothes, managing to put the offending magazine under my pants to make the caning a lot less painful as I was dragged downstairs and bent over by the Head Prefect.

A very pimply young man, with a hairstyle that was based on something from the last decadent days of Rome just before its fall, introduced a new satirical late night TV show that upset and ridiculed everything that the Establishment cherished most. He was David Frost, and along with such dangerous young hotheads as Willie Rushton, Lance Percival and Roy Kinnear, 'That Was The Week That Was' closed pubs early every Saturday night as the nation - especially the young - rushed home to enjoy the TW3 team's relentless lampooning of what our elders and supposed betters had been up to over the past seven days of their privileged lives.

David Frost and the other satire stars soon became part of a new entertainment establishment.

No. 19,600

P

The Establishment kept scoring spectacular own goals against itself, and in 1963 things finally boiled over.

The Profumo affair dominated the headlines for most of that year, where it emerged that the Minister for War - John Profumo - had had a fairly sordid liaison with a call girl, Christine Keeler. As details of the affair emerged, it became clear national security was at stake as Keeler also had business with a Soviet agent among others. It was also apparent that Profumo had lied and lied to the House of Commons. 'Private Eye' and 'That Was The Week' couldn't believe their luck, and the reporting of the trial proved how a good sex scandal could sell newspapers by the ton.

To the young it merely confirmed a growing suspicion about the hypocrisy, the deceit and double standards of the adult world.

It was the year when the Old Guard finally lost the plot. Harold Macmillan stood down, and Sir Alec Douglas Home, clearly out of touch with any real world away from the grouse moor, took over as Prime Minister; but Britain knew an election, and almost certainly an upset, was on the cards. And in America, they shot the President.

All this against the beginnings of the second great youth revolution, spearheaded in 1963 by the amazing rise of the Beatles.

That was the leak that was: Minister admits randy vice with Mandy Rice Davis (insert) and Christine Keeler.

DAILY EXPRESS

THURSDAY JUNE 6 1963

1 a.m. forecast: Sunny; thundery

Price 3d.

16

OFUMO QUITS: I LIED

He gives up War Minister's job and seat in House of Commons

His denial of impropriety with Christine K...

MOP TOP MANIA

Rock'n'roll may have seemed to have gone off the boil a bit by the beginning of what turned out to be the most exciting and revolutionary years in the history of modern music. In addition to the Fifties stars who still enjoyed nationwide popularity, the Cliff Richards, Billy Furys and Adam Faiths, there seemed to be an enormous number of popstars at the beginning of the Sixties who came and went overnight, their fancy suits in mothballs, and with very little money to show for it.

Whatever happened to Ernie K. Doe, Eden Kane, Johnny and the Hurricanes, Vince Taylor, the Ventures, Dickie Pride and the rest?....you may well ask.

Among those who did make their mark in one way or another were Chubby Checker and Rolf Harris. Chubby's main claim to fame was that he was the first person to introduce a dance form that didn't matter if you did it really badly. And most of us did just that - did it really badly. For two years Britain, along with the rest of the Western World, 'Twisted and twisted again like we did last summer'. But the Twist never really stood a chance as an exclusively teen fad, it was so easy to do (badly!) that it was practised by all age groups and people of all shapes, sizes and abilities.

Uncontrollable teenagers, intoxicated by the latest dance craze The Twist, threaten to take over television studios and vote shows like 'Juke Box Jury' and 'Ready Steady Go' a hit.

Emasculated from its rebel roots, it showed just how silly pop music had become.

Likewise, the rise of Rolf Harris to chart star status in 1960 said something about the pre-Merseybeat music scene. Under the heading 'A New Decade, A New Sound' the music press announced excitedly that Australian Rolf had given the world the Wobble Board, and his classic ditty 'Tie Me Kangaroo Down Sport' raced straight up the charts.

A Harley Street specialist has warned teenagers against doing the Twist, claiming the dance can lead to spinal displacement, loss of sexual libido and premature death. Still, you're only young once.

(There was a terrifying month of my life about three years ago - and I'm sure more frightening to Mr Harris - when I nearly moved into the house next door to Rolf in Berkshire. Still he'd have been great for coming round to help with the decorating.)

The pop business was sewn up... very few artists had the clout to dictate conditions to the Parlophones and the Deccas, and like in its pre-rock'n'roll days seemed once again to be reflecting a 'middle aged' patronising view of teenage tastes emanating from London's Tin Pan Alley.

But change was just around the corner.

Brian Birchall and his mates may not have realised it at the time, but they were in at the beginning of the youth revolution of the Sixties:

I was fifteen and working in Liverpool, I would go down to the Cavern for a lunchtime session (admission 2/6d) and stay a couple of hours and end up losing my job when I returned to work. Little did we know that the groups we saw then would be musical giants. Even at the all-nighters you couldn't buy an alcoholic drink, and we were eighteen by then.

Cinema seats all over the country suffered a worse fate than in the Bill Haley days when Beatles fans let their emotions get the better of them.

Joanna Marcus still remembers seeing, if not exactly hearing, the Beatles at the Finsbury Park Astoria:

All you could see were the heads of girls, and a nurse standing at the end of each row waiting to help those who fainted. The build-up before they came on was so intense you could almost see it. Once they came on at the end of the first half and performed a little play - a melodrama. Paul played the hero, John was the villain, George was an old lady and Ringo made a rather surreal appearance as Father Christmas, scattering snowflakes from a large basket. You couldn't hear a word they were saying for the screaming, but it still seemed to me the most hilarious thing I'd ever seen. In the second half they actually sang and played for about forty minutes.

The screaming was relentless. I stuck my fingers in my ears and joined in happily. Strangely enough, you could still hear the music in the distance behind the wall of sound, and when Paul and George shook their heads together in the 'Oohs', it seemed as if the roof was going to fly off. I thought I would explode. I've never loved anyone as much as I loved them.

Through 1960 and '61 a scruffy group of spotty scousers, with their leather clothes, winkle-picker shoes and flat fringed haircuts, looking like a cross between Beatniks and bikers, were playing a raw rock'n'roll to their first audiences in Liverpool and Hamburg. They were called the Beatles.

By 1962 they had succeeded in mesmerising the teenage population of Merseyside who thought of them as their group playing their clubs like the Cavern and the Iron Door - a literally underground scene that no one really knew about outside Liverpool and its environs. Under the wing of a shrewd young businessman called Brian Epstein, who ran a local record store and was wondering whether there was any serious money to be made in popular music, by the Spring of 1963 they had taken the country by storm, including a whole new generation of teenagers who were just young children during the rock'n'roll revolution of the mid Fifties.

This signalled the final disappearance of the old Victorian values in Britain, to be replaced in the immediate term by a youth culture of pop and fashion where anything seemed to be tolerated, the more bizarre the better. Nevertheless, in hindsight our attitudes and aspirations in 1963 were still terribly conservative.

The Beatles had their first number one hit early in the year, but by the end of the summer the squealing, sobbing scenes of deranged girls that followed them everywhere they tried to go had become absolutely commonplace.

'Beatlemania' had arrived, and with it all the old accepted standards of Tin Pan Alley pop went out of the window. It was an hysterical year for the Fab Four, at the end of which they appeared at the Royal Command Performance, where the irrepressible John Lennon failed to be overawed by the whole

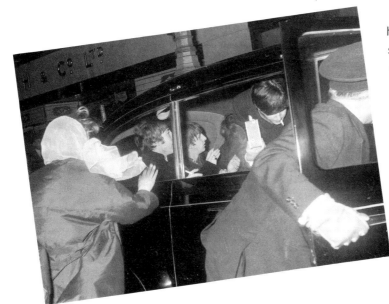

A.G. Beckett, of Warrington in Cheshire, was a member of St Paul's Youth Club, Eccles. In February 1963 they heard about a new band from Liverpool who they were keen to book for a dance. A letter to NEMS Enterprises elicited this reply:

> *NEMS ENTERPRISES LTD*
> *Directors: B. and C.J. Epstein*
>
> *6th March 1963*
>
> *Dear Sir,*
>
> *Thank you for your recent letter enquiring for the BEATLES.*
> *Whilst we would be happy to co-operate with you, we must advise that the group could not possibly play for 1 ½ hours; also, we do not feel that the fee required would be an economical proposition for your Youth Club.*
> *We do, however, handle other groups, who may already be known to you, and we have pleasure in giving you details below:*
>
> *GERRY AND THE PACEMAKERS (fee £50/60)*
> *THE BIG THREE (fee £25/30)*
> *BILLY KRAMER AND THE DAKOTAS (fee £25/30)*
>
> *Looking forward to hearing from you.*
>
> *Yours sincerely*
> *O. Johnson*

Susan Harris would have waited forever for her idols:

> *Every time there was a move at an upstairs window we were convinced it was one of them and the whole crowd erupted. My father came down there at about one in the morning with his overcoat over his pyjamas, and hauled me into the car in front of all my friends. Worst of all, I was sure Paul was peeping out of the window...*

Janet Webb saw the Beatles' influence everywhere:

 I remember going to the circus and seeing elephants wearing Beatles wigs and dancing to 'She Loves You'.

thing...'Will the people in the cheap seats clap your hands, the rest just rattle your jewellery'. By London theatre standards the audience went wild, but it was probably the only place for most of that year that they actually had to play and sing all of 'Twist And Shout'. I remember as a kid in school I got tickets to see the Beatles in concert at a theatre in Finsbury Park. I must have been one of only about seven boys in the whole soppy weeping audience. Girls were slobbering and wailing when I arrived, kept it up for a good hour and a half in the queue outside, and then got much, much worse when we got in.

Dozens of them fainted and had to be carried out on stretchers long before anybody came on stage, then they squealed non-stop for the whole of the quite short period the Beatles were actually playing - and as far as I know they are still there doing it to this day. Many of the girls seemed to me to have gone certifiably mad as they tore great tufts of their own hair out, while screaming 'John, John, George, George, oh please Paul, Paul please....' at the top of their sobbing voices. The thing I remember most vividly all these years later, apart from the fact that I certainly didn't hear a single note - in fact they could very well have not actually played one - was the unmistakable smell of girls' wee-wees. Until that extraordinary night at Finsbury Park I thought only boys did that.

At the end of 1963 no less a figure than the Observer music critic called Lennon and McCartney 'the greatest song writers since Schubert'. But did Schubert ever do Finsbury Park? - and at least after a Schubert 'gig' you could use the seats again the next day.

It was essential to the success of the Beatles' songs that they wrote them themselves. It was young peoples' music made by young people. Each new single was awaited with national excitement, and each was very different from the previous one. They were all immediate

COME BACK SOON WE'LL MISS YOU

I LOVE GEORGE

THE BEATLES QUIZ BOOK

chart-toppers; 'I Want To Hold Your Hand' sold a million inside the first three days of its release.

The commercial image of the Beatles was very much the creation of Brian Epstein, who had endless arguments with Lennon about them having to wear suits, but in the 'Yeah, Yeah, Yeah' years of '63 and '64 Brian always won, and in spite of their mop tops - at first frowned on by parents everywhere - they cultivated a 'cuddly' image that endeared them to everyone, Mums and Dads included; teenagers were already having to look elsewhere for heroes they could truly call their own.

But what the Beatles did symbolise was a new age when anything was possible, no matter who you were or where you came from. It contrasted starkly with the Britain of the late Fifties and very early Sixties, epitomised in films like 'Saturday Night and Sunday Morning' and 'A Kind Of Loving' which showed with a grainy realism the dull and still narrow-minded features of, often Northern, working-class life and morality.

POP PIRACY

For all the massive appeal of the new music that erupted in the wake of the Beatles' success, there were very few places where we could hear much of it initially. We spent hours and hours checking out the latest fab hits in little 'listening booths' in record shops, promising faithfully we were going to buy everything we heard where in truth we probably only had enough money to buy one precious single a month.

Pop radio was still on the pattern of the Fifties, the BBC Light Programme now featuring 'Saturday Club' and other beat-oriented shows, but non-stop pop was still only available from Radio Luxembourg. It only broadcast after seven-thirty in the evenings of course, but was employing new DJs including Tony Prince, David 'Kid' Jensen - whoever he was - Jimmy Young and a rambling madman called Jimmy Savile, who has been clearly raving and quite incomprehensible ever since.

Beat groups were even more anathema to parents than art school, as Bob Reed was to find out:

In 1963, aged sixteen, I was offered the chance to join a professional beat group, as they were called then. My parents refused to let me and I had to stay on at art school.

By 1964 I was in another group, again on the brink of turning professional, but had to start work in the commercial art business. I worked for a distant family relative, and great promises were made that I would be trained under his wing right up to management. But I spent the next two years in a spray booth, spraying up wooden letters for shoe-shop window displays, then I was made redundant. As a result of the long working hours and the travelling, I had to give up my group.

If Paul, John or Mick were a bit too busy for a date you might just have to make do with acned Kevin from next door and dream he looked like Alan Bates.

Even when the Beatles were 'officially' recognised with the MBE (which some thought stood for Mr Brian Epstein), the fans managed to make their investiture look more like the storming of the Bastille.

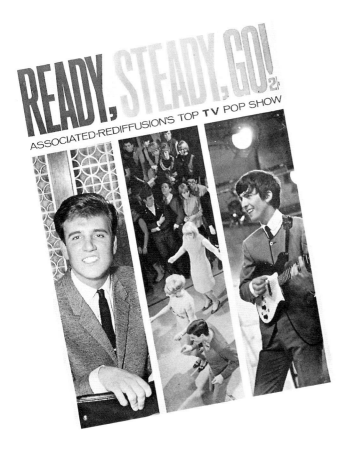

It was the offshore Pirate Radio stations that really understood the needs and the potential of the new audience, and with the arrival of Radio Caroline in 1964 we at last got what we wanted, an all day pop music station. The first week Caroline went on the air it captured seven million listeners, and within a year there were dozens of them bouncing about off the coast of the British Isles.

They featured a style that was altogether more lively and irreverent, more like American radio, than the staid announcers still used by the BBC. In the end the Pirates were beaten by a mixture of sea sickness and Government pressure, but they'd proved the potential of this kind of broadcasting and had created a whole new breed of young disc jockeys.

The obvious market for such a station was to be recognised by dear old Auntie BBC, and Radio One started up as the pirates closed down in 1967, with Tony Blackburn, Kenny Everett, Bob Holness (!!!) and John Peel, who is still there today aged 107......

With the pop boom of '63, the television chiefs were quick to provide us with new shows so we could drool over our heroes in grainy black-and-white. Following on from the Fifties success of 'Six-Five Special' and 'Oh Boy', in a very short space of time they introduced 'Juke Box Jury', 'Thank Your Lucky Stars', 'Ready Steady Go' and 'Top Of The Pops'.

'RSG' with its pop art decor, live bands and trendy presenters was undoubtedly the most teen-oriented, but sadly the more mainstream 'Top Of The Pops' is the only one that's survived till today, certainly in spite of my letters and presumably just about everyone else's.

Alan Jackson would often travel down to London to be in the studio audience for 'Ready Steady Go':

We'd spend the morning before the show scouring the trendy shops - there was one called 'I Was Lord Kitchener's Valet' - in the West End and the Portobello Road, for the old bright red military jackets that were in style. Brass buttons and epaulettes....my Dad thought I was mad, said his grandfather had thrown that kind of stuff out after the First World War!

Beryl Lomas made the trip from Stockport, Lancashire to the metropolis to see the Mecca of Mod at first hand:

The highlight came for us when we appeared in the audience of 'Ready Steady Go' shot in Wembley and hosted by Cathy McGowan, the doyenne of the Mods. She was the other style of Mod of course, long hair blunt cut with a fringe covering most of her eyes. At last we had a chance to see the London fashions at first hand. Most of the lads wore white half-mast pants with striped socks or beige jackets. The more adventurous had jackets made out of the Union Jack and nearly all of them wore casual jumpers with collars.

Sandra Thomas recalls when 'Top Of The Pops' used to come live from her native Manchester:

There would be a frantic black market in school for the free tickets. Every week there would be the top names on, the Beatles, Stones, anyone you care to mention. Consequently the shows were absolute mayhem with girls struggling to get in without tickets even after it had started.

Jimmy Savile - he was still one of our 'locals' then - and Alan Freeman were the main presenters, and they'd put a disc on in close-up like they were really playing it. Of course the groups mimed in those days, so they may as well have been just spinning the record.

Then the bigger groups started having little films of themselves playing so they didn't have the hassle of coming to the studio - I think the Beatles were first - which I suppose were the forerunners of pop videos. I think that's what made 'Ready Steady Go' much better, it was completely live in the studio.

BRITANNIA WAIVES THE RULES

I remember the mid Sixties as the one time in my life when I felt really patriotic. I suppose we all are at the bottom line, but it was a time when Britain seemed to lead the world in everything that mattered to us as teenagers; pop, fashion and for one unforgettable year even football. Mary Quant was selling huge quantities of her affordable and expendable clothes on both sides of the Atlantic. Union Jacks were sewn onto anything and everything, and Liverpool and Carnaby Street were the two most famous places on earth.

It was the time of Harold Wilson's 'I'm Backing Britain' campaign, and like everything else in the mid Sixties, patriotism had gone pop.

And it did seem, briefly, that teen rebellion might have gone off the boil.

The thing we took the greatest national pride in was the colossal scale of the Beatles' conquest of America. No British artists had ever quite made the leap across the Atlantic, but the Fab Four took the States by storm and paved the way for an armada of British groups to make it in the USA.

After hysterical arrival scenes at the airport and a crucial appearance on the Ed Sullivan TV show, the Beatles were virtually given the freedom of America. On 4th April 1964 the US Billboard chart showed them at numbers 1, 2, 3, 4, 5, 31, 41, 46, 58, 65, 68 and 79. Quite simply, they were the most popular people in the world.

And this week's Window On The World takes us to swinging London; no more trailing round the Tower or meandering down the Mall for the trendy tourist - the place to head for is colourful Carnaby Street, where the new has ousted the old as the city's main attraction....

It was 1965 when Wilson - officially the Queen of course - awarded the Beatles the MBE, which immediately sparked off a storm among a lot of the older recipients who sent them back in disgust. Likewise, Lennon also outraged the Rolls Royce company by hand painting his brand new Roller in his own hectic colour scheme.

All very puzzling. It always seemed to me that if you could afford to fork out that sort of money for a car, then it was yours to keep goats in if you wished.

LIKE A ROLLING STONE

The time was ripe for the arrival on the scene of another group that we could really horrify our Mums and Dads with, and right on cue manager Andrew Loog Oldham appeared with the Rolling Stones.

The Stones had absolutely everything that parents could instantly hate, and we could latch on to as our own. They had longer hair than ever seen before, were ugly, unshaven, and clearly hadn't had a bath in months. That was the image anyway, and when I switched allegiances on my Dansette Major record player from 'Help' and 'Hard Days' Night' to 'Not Fade Away' and 'Satisfaction', my Dad was convinced I'd finally flipped and would almost certainly end up in jail if not on the gibbet.

Not only didn't they wear suits, even the rather odd Mao Tse Tung suits that the Beatles had adopted, but they didn't even wear ties. Jagger used to sport a strange grey crew neck jumper underneath a jacket, with no shirt or tie, a style I immediately took to, if only 'cos I hated doing knots.

'*Local bikes go topless as bobbies get to bottom of boutique publicity prank!*'

77

Oldham sussed that the more scandal that surrounded the Stones, the more money they would rake in. Jagger and co were banned from hotels, caused punch-ups, were even arrested for urinating in public. Fathers were particularly anti-Jagger, because not only did he clearly threaten to deflower their darling daughters, and probably did - or at least tried to - but there was also a strange strutting effeminacy in the way he moved and postured that threatened the very fabric of everything decent, manly and straight.

The more middle-aged Britain hated and despised the Stones, and middle-aged by now seemed to mean anyone over about twenty-eight, the more their teenage fans would worship them, buy their records and queue for hours around the block to see them in concert.

By now I was wearing my own hair daringly long and had actually cut my own fringe into a sort of deranged monk style, all done very skilfully in the bath with nail scissors. Dad thought I looked a total pillock and I think on balance he was probably right.

One Friday night, having queued for an hour to see the Stones at the Ricky Tick club in Windsor, I was told I couldn't come in 'cos I looked too scruffy. The fact that compared with Keith Richards I looked like James Bond cut no ice with a particularly large bouncer, so I had to slink away ashamed. I came back the next night with a silly hat on and got in straight away. I drank something like eighteen pints for about two pounds, learnt to do a new dance called the Nod and sang 'Little Red Rooster' all the way home in Tubby Thompson's beaten up old Ford Popular.

My first move was to get a *Rolling Stone* as a boyfriend.
I slept with three of them, then decided the lead singer was
the best.

Marianne Faithfull

Val Roberts remembers the Stones appearing in Prestatyn, North Wales:

They were advertised as 'London's Answer To The Beatles', but looked a lot scruffier. I think they just wore jeans and baggy sweaters, unheard of on stage in those days. And their hair wasn't just long, it looked greasy. When I came home clutching a photo of them, my Mum asked if I'd been to the zoo.....

Their energetic performances and songwriting talents have kept them at the top for over a quarter of a century, but at the time the mood of British youth was absolutely right for the Stones.

Along with all the other British bands - Gerry and the Pacemakers, the Searchers, Dave Clark, Herman's Hermits and so on, the Rolling Stones became hugely successful in America for exactly the same reason as in the UK, because parents hated them and Dads in particular wanted to have them publicly castrated.

They then went on to commit the ultimate outrage the next year on British television. In front of a shocked and disbelieving nation they refused to wave to the audience on the revolving stage at the end of 'Sunday Night at the London Palladium'. Unspeakable. They should certainly have been horse-whipped and thrown into the Tower.

Bob Reed's boycott of the barbershops of Dartford was typical:

In the Fifties we had had to put up with short back and sides just like our Dads'. In the early Sixties the Beatles and the Rolling Stones arrived with long, and what our parents considered, unwashed hair. Our short back and sides became less short, with the expected reaction from parents.

TALKIN' 'BOUT MY GENERATION

In spite of the carefully cultivated uncultivated look of Mick and the boys, bands like the Stones and The Who soon gave rise to a fashion very different from the mop tops and neat collarless suits of the Beatles. The Mods began to appear, initially in London, with an obsession about looking trendy and sharp that men hadn't really had. Apart from the Ted phase, young male fashion was never much of a market - you simply bought a suit like your Dad's only smaller and hopefully cheaper. That and a couple of jumpers would do most British blokes for several years.

Initially a London minority of obsessive fashion freaks who followed Rhythm and Blues bands and Modern Jazz, within a few months in 1964 the 'Look' was being copied all over Britain, wherever young guys had money to spare in their pockets.

They sported flared trousers and immaculately back-combed hairstyles, and spent most of their wages every weekend on clothes and petrol for their ubiquitous scooters with Moddy girls hanging on the back in their angular Vidal Sassoon haircuts. They delighted in their new clothes having what excitable salesmen called 'planned obsolescence', which meant basically that they didn't cost a lot which was lucky because they'd fall apart extremely quickly in any case.

Their rebellion was truly teenage in that it was about generations rather than society - they didn't mind work, consumerism and so on, but simply despised anyone not of their age group. They worshipped the Who with their 'Hope to die before I grow old' philosophy, who lived and behaved on stage as if planned obsolescence was built into their little Moddy bodies as well as their hipster flared trousers.

Brian Birchall recalls Mods on Merseyside:

The Mods, with their Parka coats with the Who motif on the back and their Vespas, would congregate at the Pier Head with their girlfriends. The girls had Mary Quant style haircuts, pan-stick make-up and eyes like Dusty Springfield, thick with black mascara. It was as if they had their own uniforms.

After weekends spent in dark, sweat-oozing cellars, all Madras jackets and pill-popping energy, and blasted by bands such as The Who or the Action, you didn't need make-up to look like a Mod on Monday.

Reddish, Stockport, had its quota of Mods, including Beryl Lomas:

In the mid Sixties my friends and I decided to become Mods and sported hair cropped to ¼ inch all over and black, Panda eye make-up. Our faces and lips were deathly pale courtesy of some over zealous powdering and we wore suits with straight skirts, white tights and lace-up suede shoes. These were coupled with the obligatory blue nylon macs, plain sweaters and stud earrings. Of course we had the scooters, Lambrettas with dozens of mirrors and (for the boys) compulsory Parkas and pork pie hats.

A nasty side-effect for the rest of us during the whole Mod era was that they all got their little Lambrettas out every bank holiday, popped on the ritual Parka and zoomed off mob-handed to places as sleepy as Clacton, Margate and Hastings to spend an entire weekend beating lumps out of any Rockers who were silly enough to be coming the other way. Of course inevitably the Rockers themselves started to organise, and began to come the other way in equally large numbers, tooled up and ready for a rumble, and for two summers it became a gentleman's occasion at weekends. There were many arrests, and the lines seemed drawn once again between teenagers and the rest.

One real problem during the Mods and Rockers period was trying to act and dress neutrally. Plain clothes members of both factions would saunter up to you in the street and say menacingly ''Ere, mate, what are you, a Mod or a Rocker?'. If you gave the wrong reply, they beat you up. When the same question was once asked of the Beatles, John Lennon replied 'We're just Mockers'.

TOO FAST TO LOVE...

'England swings like a pendulum do....' sang Roger Miller; I was in Birmingham in the mid Sixties and still not sure what was so swinging about them. Apart from the music and the arrival of mini skirts, there wasn't a whole hell of a lot of swinging going on in the suburban streets of Selly Oak. We just drank our way through another year.

The newspapers were full of it though. There was a sense of another world happening down the other end of the MI. A world where all the girls went 'all the way' all the time, where everybody drove Mini Cooper S's and drank on the Kings Road with Jean Shrimpton and Cathy McGowan. There was a whole new

wave of instant personalities - Vidal Sassoon, Mary Quant, Ozzie Clark and the meteoric Simon Dee. Simon Dee was the embodiment of everything the marketing men wanted to project about the Sixties. He arrived for his chat show every week in *the* E-Type, with *the* Fab Groovy shirt, *the* long-legged dollybird hanging almost everything she'd got out over the side of the car, while Simon came on and did us all the enormous favour of being on our screens. Sadly Simon appeared to believe this nonsense himself and disappeared even more quickly than he had arrived.

In April 1966 'Time' magazine announced Swinging London as an official fact. It had actually been swinging for a couple of years, at least in areas such as the Kings Road, Chelsea, but the 'Time' report was an acknowledgement that these rather loud long-haired young people represented a thriving youth-based economy in Britain that was leading the world.

By now the main London fashion centres had moved across the city. Carnaby Street had become more of a tourist trap than a serious shopping area, and shops like 'Granny Takes a Trip' were doing better business in Chelsea, Kensington and the Portobello Road.

It was the year when every girl in the country wore a mini skirt, whether the shape of her legs could stand it or not, and a lot clearly couldn't. And the Mini was still the car of the Sixties. Everybody seemed to own one. The rich and famous had them for ease of parking in London's busy streets, with black windows and floral paintschemes. The rest of us made do with battered old second-hand ones.

The Mods would use 'pep pills' to keep awake at all-night club sessions, as Cathy Paul of Blackburn remembers:

> We'd go to the Twisted Wheel in Manchester for the Saturday allnighter. There'd be four or five groups on, soul and R&B, and sometimes you couldn't get in the toilets without wading through a sea of Coke and 'prellies' (preludin). The Coke was all you could get to drink, so it was mainly used to wash down dozens of prellies.

Mods-on-wheels never really had the style of their Rocker rivals, the Vespa hardly a match for the Vincent or the Harley.

'Battle of the Bank Holiday beaches as Mods and Rockers descend on Margate and Brighton!'. All leave was cancelled for the local constabulary and the general public were told to lock up their daughters.

Anything goes, even mini-skirts for men. That's the philosophy of Sixties' fashion. Tricia Reed certainly didn't believe in the conventional white wedding dress:

> *I ended the Sixties by getting married at Gravesend Registry Office. It was quite unusual in those days to get married in a Registry Office, a church service was the done thing. I don't think my grandmother who was a devout Catholic ever forgave me. I wore a blue mini dress and a big, wide-brimmed hat. My make-up was very pale and emphasized by my double thick Mary Quant eyelashes. My hair was flicked up on each side - just like Lulu. My husband Bob wore a leather jacket with a floral tie and beige hipster trousers.*

Chris Pope caught the do-it-yourself bug in customised fashion:

> *Woolworth's was the place to buy small pots of powdered dye. I remember collecting pebbles and tying them tightly with string into an old T-shirt and faded jeans. I tie-dyed them orange and wore them together all summer.*

C.S. Atkins was obviously the Dedicated Follower of Fashion as far as Dursley, Gloucestershire, was concerned:

> *Unless you were a bike-less biker usual clothes were a pastel shade tab shirt or black, roll-necked sweater, ice blue or denim jeans, black cuban heeled boots, and if you were really lucky, a fake suede 'Beatle' jacket. Man weren't we cool striding through town with a Lucky Strike dangling from our lips.*

...TOO YOUNG TO TIE-DYE

In this explosion of teenage consumerism, often the only expression of rebellion was in the outrageous nature of what one consumed one way or another, be it in clothes, music or whatever. I bought a particularly tasteless Union Jack suit, and was convinced that I looked fabulous. I also bought the widest pair of flared hipster trousers I could find anywhere in Reading. They flapped about my ankles as I walked and nearly caused my untimely end when they got stuck at the end of an escalator in the John Lewis store. I was lucky to escape with no worse damage than a great chunk gouged out of one flare which I immediately conned a girlfriend into patching up in a yellow polka dot material that she was going to use for her little flat in Edgbaston. The trousers are long gone, although I can't imagine who would have wanted them, probably the local Oxfam; but on occasion when in the Midlands I pass that little flat and all these years later it's still got just the one yellow polka dot curtain hanging across one side of the window. The rest went up my trouser leg.

Patches of course were a great part of our student economy. Levi's were the only jeans worth even

While rockstars flaunted their fortunes with flowers, the Bubblecar made a brief appearance urging the rest of us to 'Go To Work In An Egg'.

contemplating being seen in, they were soaked in a hot bath with us still inside them, to get them as tight as possible, bleached, then patched and patched over again until none of the original denim was left anywhere, just the all-important Levi Strauss badge on the back right pocket, and of course the little red tag. Most of us bought our Levi's straight legged, but then cut them up the seam from the ankle and sewed a patch into a big V shape at the bottom of each leg to make them flare. We usually conned a girlfriend with a sewing machine into doing all our gentlemen's tailoring, although a particularly stupid mate of mine from Elstree did his own instant flared bottoms on his jeans....so he was the only swinging Londoner wearing Levi's with a wide upside-down Paisley flare at the knee, tapering down again at the ankle. He thought he looked totally cool and groovy, we all thought he looked like a total pillock.

BRINGIN' IT ALL BACK HOME

As students we were particularly aware of whispers coming over from an increasingly troubled America, where they were getting deeper and deeper involved in the no-win war situation in Vietnam, of student unrest, of widespread racial tensions and an increase in the use of hallucinogenic drugs.

After the initial wholesome surfing sounds of the Beach Boys early in the decade, the trauma of the Kennedy assassination left a gap which was filled to a degree by the British invasion, but just as significantly by the whole 'protest song' movement led by Bob Dylan.

As social problems intensified, Dylan emerged as the mouthpiece of disgruntled youth with anthems like 'Blowing In The Wind' and 'A Hard Rain's Gonna Fall'. By the mid Sixties, he had moved away from political protest to articulate the disenchantment of a generation with like 'Like A Rolling Stone' and 'Subterranean Homesick Blues'. To others he was just a whining folkie with a frustrated rocker struggling to get out.

'Society's thin blue line of law and order is becoming increasingly strained under pressure from the disenchanted young, an anger fuelled by the Vietnam conflict and the radical message of much popular music.'

Local magistrate after anti-Vietnam demo

Jack Sanders was one of the last of the 'Grammar School' kids in Newcastle before they all went Comprehensive:

We really thought we were 'with it' because we'd discovered Bob Dylan before the rest. I suppose we were Tyneside's first hippies, sitting round a record player smoking pot and thinking how profound the lyrics were.

'Don't follow leaders
Watch the parkin' meters.'
Bob Dylan, 'Subterranean Homesick Blues'

Feeling grew against the war, and a counter-culture built up of thousands of young people who rejected everything that straight society stood for, opting to drop out altogether. Protest against the war spread across the US as reports came back from south-east Asia of heavy civilian casualties, innocent mothers and their babies getting caught up in the hunt for the Vietcong, and the use of torture, terror bombing and napalm. There were half a million servicemen out in the jungles of Vietnam by 1967, and most of them were teenagers.

More and more body bags were flown back home every day. Many people just wanted to get young Americans out of the war because they could see their army getting bogged down for years, achieving very little and costing hundreds of thousands of lives. Others felt they had no quarrel with the Vietnamese. Boxer Mohammed Ali refused point blank to fight in Vietnam and said 'No Vietcong ever called me nigger!'.

Kids on both sides of the Atlantic knew the slogans by heart: 'LBJ, LBJ, how many kids did you kill today..?', and of course 'Make Love Not War'.

The feeling against the war, and the involvement of people like Joan Baez, Ali and Norman Mailer, turned into a rejection of the society that ever allowed such a war to start, and young people began to question their attitude to the family unit, sexuality and - most significantly as it turned out - sexual equality.

DOLLY ROCKERS

It was 1966 when Mary Quant decided pubic hair might be the latest fashion feature and proudly told us all that she'd had her pubes cut into the shape of a heart. I don't know if it was true, and sadly never got to find out, but if she had had it done, it would of course have had to have been done by Vidal Sassoon, who somehow had wormed

There was a time when every girl under twenty yearned to look an experienced, sophisticated thirty. Suddenly every girl wants to look under the age of consent.

Mary Quant

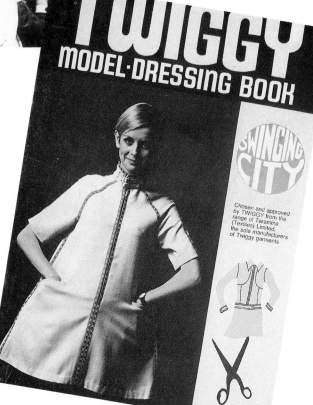

his way into position as *the* Hairdresser for swinging Londoners, in the same way that David Bailey was *the* Photographer and a funny little six-and-a-half-stone East End waif was *the* Model. Her face stared at us from every magazine, and she was the symbol of everything the youth revolution had done in the fashion scene.

Very tiny with a real 'Gor Blimey' accent, cropped hair and a figure like Olive Oyl, Twiggy was about as far from the elegant 'frightfully frightfully' debutantes that used to float down the catwalks as it was possible to be.

Her elevation to celebrity status was another demonstration of what was possible for a simple working-class kid to achieve in this decade of opportunity. 'Twig's' rise to fame was a typical Sixties success story. If it could happen to Leslie Hornby it could happen to anybody. She was rumoured to earn as much as ten guineas in a single hour....

Women may have been making money, but they weren't making much headway against what was still a very male controlled Britain. The Pill had given them a

MENS
POP
WIGS

100% REAL HAIR

Please send me wig style A / B / C /or D
attached cutting (or state colour requi
of £14 14s 0d which includes

Name...............

Addre
....

I enclos

To: Kyla

Pop fans! Make sure you're really 'with it' with the very latest pop-art and op-art fashions in dynamic day-glo colours, straight from London's swinging Kings Road.

CAT
GIRL
TIGHTS

by Wolsey

Every student bedsit was a potential hive of cocoa sipping plotters intent upon the overthrow of civilisation as we know it.

choice of whether or not they wanted to have a baby, it had put women in charge of contraception for the first time, but it also gave men less to be responsible about.

The old fear of having to marry a girl if you 'got her into trouble' more or less disappeared with the arrival of the Pill, and it meant men could often treat women even more badly than before.

In America women seemed to be organising as Feminists for the first time, but in Britain the girls that hung on the arms of pop stars, the Marianne Faithfulls and Jane Ashers, all looked the part with long straight hair and long straight legs up to their navels, but they weren't ever really asked their opinions on anything, or expected by the media to have any.

My own love life was typically chauvinist. I drank whenever I wanted, which was more or less all the time. I went fishing for most of the rest of the time, and girlfriends had to fit in with that. Most of them preferred not to fit in with it at all, or stick it for a while convinced they'd change me. Then they'd realise that I was past praying for, and would go off as abruptly as they'd arrived.

I did occasionally make pathetic attempts at compromise, but they were always doomed to total failure. The most disastrous episode when trying to combine fishing and a romantic evening with a new girlfriend was when I took a particularly beautiful blond mini-skirted lady across Reading in my Mini van, not telling her the reason for our trip. 'Just a drive' was all I could mumble unconvincingly.

Well how would you tell a gorgeous eighteen year-old in a yellow mini dress that you had to collect a huge plastic dustbin full of steaming oxblood for fishing later that night? Somehow I did brilliantly manage to smuggle it into the van without her sussing why I had to park outside Reading Abattoir, but what I didn't allow for was a sweet little old lady who suddenly stepped off the kerb and right in front of my Mini as I raced across town.

I stomped on the brakes, the little old lady carried on across the road as if nothing had happened, and the bucket of steaming, frothing oxblood took off up out of the back seat and all over the golden hair and elegant summer outfit of the new lady. It looked like something from 'Nightmare On Elm Street'. She sobbed, she screamed, she raged at me, and shamefacedly I have to admit the more she sobbed the worse I got the giggles. In the end she became quite hysterical and I had to take her to her Mum's for a bath and change of clothes.

Once I'd managed to explain that her only daughter hadn't actually been involved in a major road crash or attacked by the Mad Axeman, I have to say her Mum wasn't too understanding. She shut the door on me with a look of pure hatred, while I could hear her daughter upstairs still sobbing while running the bath. Puzzlingly she didn't call and I never ever did see her again. And that night I went fishing....

HAIR TODAY

What was becoming increasingly noticeable in the middle of the decade was that the clear differences between men and women were breaking down.

The anything-goes style of men's fashion, the universal wearing of jeans by both sexes and the ever-increasing length of men's hair meant it was getting harder and harder to tell the sexes apart.

Many a male motorist experienced the red-faced embarrassment of pulling up to offer a shapely looking girl a lift at a bus stop only to have her turn and find she was a man. And the already disturbing un-macho Jagger further

The most unlikely of young tearaways would take time out from the mad social whirl of swinging England with the soul-enhancing sport of fishing.

Paul Laver's transformation from shy, awkward teenager to Sixties rebel was brought about by a trip to a concert at the Corn Exchange in Bristol:

I went to the toilet and as I was combing my hair in the mirror two men walked in. At first I thought they were girls. They wore high-necked Paisley shirts buttoned down at the collar, checked jackets with very long vents, and black, flared trousers with very high Cuban heels. They reminded me of 18th-century dandies. I was knocked out by the look. The two men were Ray and Dave Davies of The Kinks. The music they played was raw and so different to anything I had heard before. In a short space of time I too became a rebel, dressed in a Guard's jacket with gold epaulettes, silver crushed velvet trousers, white plimsolls and fur gloves. I even found a girlfriend.

Cool soon became kitsch as commercialism inevitably got in on the act. Janet Webb of Lincoln remembers the bells'n'beads:

Hippy bells were 2-3 inches high and wide and painted in bright colours and hung on a long gold cord round your neck. You wore them with long floppy clothes, a floppy hat, long waistcoats and bell-bottomed jeans which had to be frayed at the hem. You had flowers, love and peace emblems and Ethiopian crosses embroidered on everything.

Rod Jones experienced frequent rebuffs when he donned his hippy gear:

I was calling at a girlfriend's house, wearing a Paisley shirt, beads, and sporting a wisp of a moustache. Her big brother opened the door, looked me up and down, and shouted over his shoulder 'I think it's for you....it's Sgt. Pepper!'

alarmed Britain's fathers by appearing with all the other Rolling Stones on an album cover in full drag.

Long hair became more emotive with our parents than any other single issue. We grew our hair to express our individuality and yet we all looked the same. The more our parents hated it long, the more we let it grow. My Mum used to make subtle suggestions like 'Wouldn't nice short be more suitable for swimming, easier to dry?'. When I pointed out that I hadn't had the slightest inclination to go swimming for the past four or five years, she would think of something else like fear of headlice, or rats wanting to nest in it.

Inevitably, things could be a lot more extreme elsewhere.

In Greece, the take-over by the Colonels in a military coup signalled the banning of all mini skirts on girls and long hair on men. On a very unrebellious holiday to the Costa del Sol I found myself locked up for two nights in a Spanish jail just for having shoulder-length hair. While in the States, men's hair just got longer and longer.

PEACE'N'LOVE, MAN...

The hippy movement grew out the American anti-war movement, teenagers all over the US 'tuning in, turning on and dropping out' as they left their suburban homes by the thousand making for the Haight-Ashbury district of San Francisco or even setting up tribal-style communes of their own. Once the top rock names had embraced the idea as part of the 'Beautiful People' (who had little dropping out to do as they didn't need to work anyway) the psychedelic era caught on in Britain as well.

They made love freely with whoever they liked, where and when they liked, and they experimented with drugs like LSD and marijuana. Drugs were promoted as the light to some mystical inner truth, but in reality they were just something else to try and lift another boring wet Wednesday. There was an awful lot of claptrap talked by almost everybody.

'The Flower Children Are Big Business!
They dress in exotic costumes, bludgeon their senses with cacophonous music and wild flashing lights, are pacifists, exhibitionists and layabouts....and their cult is growing daily.'

By 1968 if you had any pretensions to rebellion you were either out of your head on the Isle of Wight or in a head to head confrontation with the law. Eddie Harrison was a student activist at East Anglia University, Norwich:

> We had moved away from the peace and love of IT (International Times) with its flying saucers and magic mushrooms, to a paper called Black Dwarf which seemed to urge armed insurrection on every other page. It happened for real in Paris for a few days, but elsewhere was mostly just wishful thinking.

Phil Thomas helped organise a sit-in at Hornsey College of Art:

> I don't think we really knew what we wanted, except change. When we went to Grosvenor Square we thought it was going to be the beginning of the Revolution. We shouted 'Ho, Ho, Ho Chi Min' in praise of the North Vietnamese leader, my girlfriend even had a carrier bag designed as a Vietcong flag, but the day just ended up in running battles with the fuzz that petered out once the telly cameras had left.

Oliver Martin was an ambitious hitchhiker who'd backpacked to the East in '68:

> I took the 'hippy trail' to Kathmandu, I was just eighteen, my parents didn't know where I was for nearly a year. Then I did the States in 1969 and was there when Woodstock was announced. I managed to get there a day late....all I found was a sea of mud and hundreds of stragglers, like the aftermath of some medieval battle.

The Beatles regained their street credibility as rebel role models when the moptops admitted they were now Day Trippers of a different kind. But Maharishi Yogi turned out to be a bit of a boo-boo!

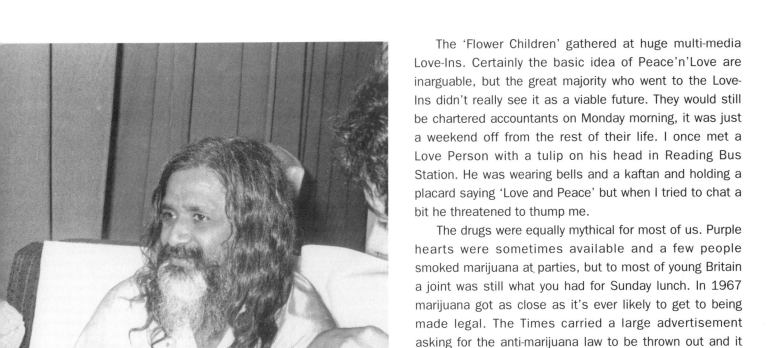

The 'Flower Children' gathered at huge multi-media Love-Ins. Certainly the basic idea of Peace'n'Love are inarguable, but the great majority who went to the Love-Ins didn't really see it as a viable future. They would still be chartered accountants on Monday morning, it was just a weekend off from the rest of their life. I once met a Love Person with a tulip on his head in Reading Bus Station. He was wearing bells and a kaftan and holding a placard saying 'Love and Peace' but when I tried to chat a bit he threatened to thump me.

The drugs were equally mythical for most of us. Purple hearts were sometimes available and a few people smoked marijuana at parties, but to most of young Britain a joint was still what you had for Sunday lunch. In 1967 marijuana got as close as it's ever likely to get to being made legal. The Times carried a large advertisement asking for the anti-marijuana law to be thrown out and it wasn't just rock stars, disc jockeys and other riff raff that gave the campaign to change the law their support, but such respected members of society as Brian Walden, MP David Dimbleby, Graham Greene and even Norman St John Stevas.

In spite of such unlikely bedfellows the campaign never quite mustered enough support, and in the meantime the purges against drug takers continued with the full might of the law behind them. Rolling Stones Mick Jagger and Brian Jones were both found guilty of possession of drugs, and given jail sentences. This seemed unnecessarily harsh even to the Stones' fiercest critics, and the sentences were thrown out on

Away from the 'happenings' in 1967, life was a pretty fruitless search for the psychedelic experience as Brian Hall remembers:

Alan Ginsberg may have been chanting mantras in Hyde Park for legalising pot but in Leicester none of us had a clue how to get hold of the stuff let alone what to do with it. However, rumours did go around about the hallucinogenic qualities of quite ordinary foodstuffs like banana skins. You were supposed to dry them in the oven and smoke them. We had an abortive attempt one afternoon when my Mum was out shopping, but turned the oven up to high and ended up with a little pile of cinders. My Mum was impressed though, she thought her son was taking up cookery!

'Britain's youth goes potty' screamed the tabloids as marijuana mania apparently swept out of control, flooding the streets with cannabis, pot, charge, grass, bush, hash, draw, reefers, joints, spliffs, skins, roaches...you name it, we tried it.

appeal. The Times carried an article deploring the excessive reaction of the legal system to Jagger and Jones, asking 'Who breaks a butterfly on a wheel?'.

And of course it made the errant Stones true martyrs to the continuing rebellion of youth.

The Beatles by this time had shed their clean-cut boy-next-door appeal. They were long haired, bearded and very much influenced in the Flower Power era by drugs, mysticism and meditation. They had performed their last ever public concert in August '66, they were just too big, too famous to appear anywhere anymore, but in June '67 released their greatest ever work, the 'Sergeant Pepper' album; they also made the anthem of the era, 'All You Need Is Love'. Later that same summer of '67 they got involved with the Indian guru Maharishi Mahesh Yogi, while at the same time their long-time mentor and guiding light Brian Epstein - who had become increasingly lonely, paranoid, erratic and drug dependent - killed himself.

It was the era that saw the first of the great open-air concerts, rallying points for the culture of youth, at Monterey, Hyde Park and so on. If public sympathy was still divided over long hair, drugs, kaftans and communes, it recognised it was certainly one of the most creative periods for musicians, with Cream, Pink Floyd, Jimi Hendrix all making their mark at the time.

SOMETHING IN THE AIR

The last years of the Sixties saw a lot of positive liberal ideas come to fruition.

There was a new law legalising abortion, that up until then had been a sordid and dangerous backstreet affair; in spite of the increased availablity of contraception many births were still unplanned.

MP Leo Abse introduced a new law to legalise homosexuality in Britain, and in the States the word 'gay' was used for the first time in the media to describe

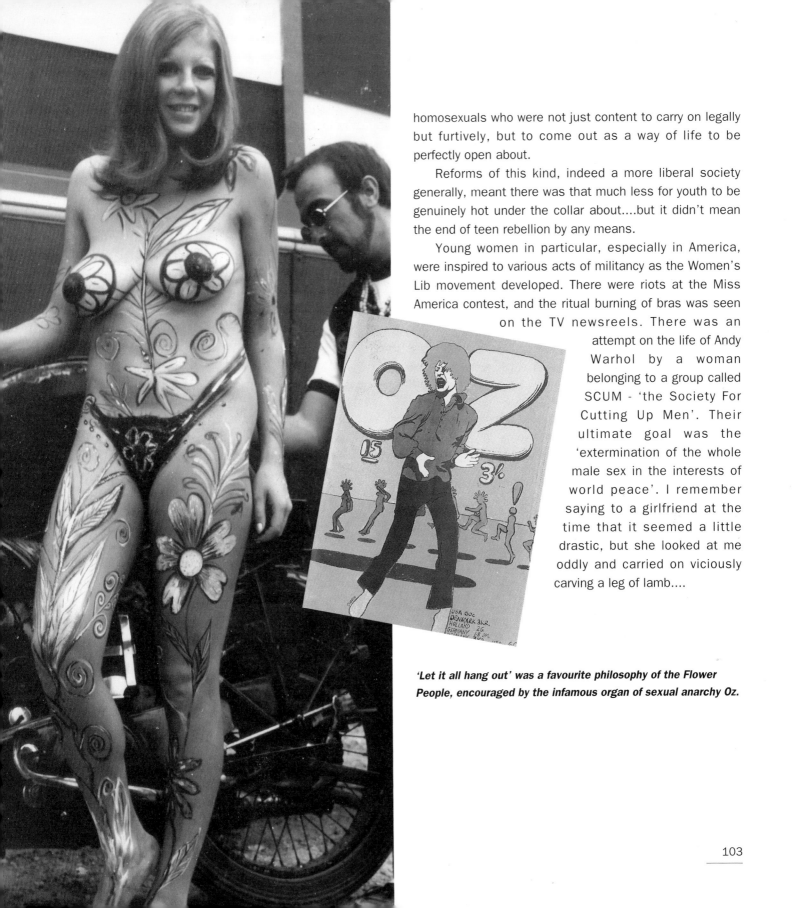

homosexuals who were not just content to carry on legally but furtively, but to come out as a way of life to be perfectly open about.

Reforms of this kind, indeed a more liberal society generally, meant there was that much less for youth to be genuinely hot under the collar about....but it didn't mean the end of teen rebellion by any means.

Young women in particular, especially in America, were inspired to various acts of militancy as the Women's Lib movement developed. There were riots at the Miss America contest, and the ritual burning of bras was seen on the TV newsreels. There was an attempt on the life of Andy Warhol by a woman belonging to a group called SCUM - 'the Society For Cutting Up Men'. Their ultimate goal was the 'extermination of the whole male sex in the interests of world peace'. I remember saying to a girlfriend at the time that it seemed a little drastic, but she looked at me oddly and carried on viciously carving a leg of lamb....

'Let it all hang out' was a favourite philosophy of the Flower People, encouraged by the infamous organ of sexual anarchy Oz.

Mass Love-Ins gave way to the less tempting Sit-Ins as things got all political and serious towards the end of the decade.

'WE WILL FIGHT, WE WILL WIN, PARIS LONDON ROME BERLIN.....'

1968 was the year of student revolt across the world.

While America was racked with riots in the black ghettos and mounting demands for an end to the Vietnam war, bitter anger about the status quo finally boiled over everywhere. There were student-led riots and strikes in France, Germany, Italy, Poland, Czechoslovakia, Mexico and Japan as well as college occupations and scenes like the Grosvenor Square demonstrations in the UK.

The headlines were filled with Rudi Dutschke, Daniel Cohn-Bendit and Tariq Ali. Tear gas and baton charges were familiar pictures on the newsreels from around the world. By 22nd May in France the revolution had spread from the Sorbonne to the whole working class, and ten million Frenchmen went on general strike.

The hands were removed from the clocks in Paris in a gesture meaning 'no more time'...presumably therefore no more work, and no more money.

The universities and colleges had been too restrictive for too long, many were totally out of touch with student needs. They were still extraordinarily prissy. Even in the enlightened, permissive Britain of the late Sixties, in many universities it was still against the rules to 'entertain' members of the opposite sex in your room even in the daytime. And to the average twenty-year-old this was plain daft.

Some of the more fanatical student activists had visions of forcing a total breakdown of the Old Order and setting up revolutionary governments around the world, but most of us had no such clear ideology. We just had a basic anti-authoritarianism, and were fed up with being pushed around by people we couldn't respect. The other problem of course was that we actually rather liked the aggro. It was exciting. Jagger was quoted at the time as saying violence gave him 'a buzz', and the Stones album 'Street Fighting Man' was banned in the USA for being likely to incite trouble.

Of all the things likely to cause riots in the States, Mick'n'Keef seemed to be the least of their problems. The ghettoes had become completely no-go areas; Chicago was more or less in open civil war. The more militant black groups were turning on the moderates, while Martin Luther King and Robert Kennedy were both murdered within a few weeks of each other. And Nixon was elected to the White House.

And this just a year after the Summer of Love....

THE DREAM IS OVER?

The Hippy culture was still strong in the US and over here, but it was finding it hard to survive in the real world of declining economies, the escalating horror of Vietnam and a realisation of some of the dangers of drug use. Finally there were the Sharon Tate murders at the hands of Charles Manson and his demonic 'family', an incident that sent shivers down the spine of the young.

Yet in the main for those of us who survived the course, the Sixties ended on a series of high notes. Man finally walked on the moon, though I'm not sure what it achieved. Unlike Raleigh and co who brought something tangible back from the New World like turkey and spuds - a complete Christmas dinner in fact, and a smoke afterwards - Armstrong and crew didn't actually bring home anything except big superfit crewcut smiles and some dust.

The great festivals of Love, Music and Peace saw out the decade with Woodstock and the Isle of Wight - which featured Bob Dylan live again after Bob Dylan had been wherever Bob Dylan goes - and the Stones organised the free concert in Hyde Park. Sadly it was three days too late for Brian Jones, who died mysteriously in a swimming pool, amid rumours of drug-taking and suicide.

Most of us were just 'weekend hippies'. Maureen Connolly took the bus from Leeds to take part in a 'Love Festival' at London's UFO Club:

It was all very psychedelic - light shows, everybody smoking joints and waving joss sticks about, some on LSD no doubt, people writhing around on the floor, the music almost unbearably loud. Then my friend and I went backstage to talk to one of the groups, and noticed the musicians were more interested in stocking up on crates of beer from their van...

'...we walked into Jimi's dressing room making our intentions very obvious, only to find he already had a couple of girls on each arm - he didn't even notice we were there. We trudged home in the rain, our fantasies shattered....failed groupies'.

The circus was over. Like redundant clowns, most of the Flower Children wiped off the greasepaint and got on with real life, though a few of us stuck at it in overcrowded squats around Notting Hill and windswept communes in Wales.

There was a serious end to the Sixties for Eileen Jamison and her Saturday afternoon sessions in the dark and smokey basement of Belfast's Pound Music Club:

Alas the troubles struck Belfast in 1969 and one of my last memories of the Pound was sitting one Saturday afternoon with the sound of gunfire echoing outside and all within, Protestant and Catholic, singing 'Give Peace a Chance'. It was a poignant moment.

The Beatles ended the Sixties, symbolically, by breaking up, while John and Yoko said goodbye to the decade in their own style of rebellion by staging the Bed In For Peace at the Amsterdam Hilton.

The Americans finally started to withdraw from Vietnam; by the end many of the troops were drug crazed and in open rebellion, an estimate in 1968 found that over half the personnel smoked marijuana and over ten percent were occasional users of heroin. Horrific facts started to emerge about the massacre at My Lai and other atrocities against the civilian population committed by young Americans.

As America started to extricate itself from Vietnam, the British Army found itself increasingly involved in Northern Ireland...the Soviets invaded Czechoslovakia, Palestinians hijacked an Israeli airliner...there was famine in a place called Biafra...and the world continued to turn.

Colour came to all the British TV channels at last, just in time to see how pretty Terry Gilliam's cartoons were on a rather strange new show called 'Monty Python's Flying Circus'.

The movie 'If' had public schoolboys in armed revolt against the Establishment - teachers, parents, church, the lot - and poor downtrodden little Hooray Henrys cheered wildly in cinemas all over the country.

And there was the film of D.H. Lawrence's 'Women In Love' which had very different effects on different audiences. I first saw it in one of those too-arty-for-their-own-good Academy cinemas in Oxford Street. At the point where Oliver Reed and Alan Bates stripped off and started wrestling, the audience who had been sitting in hushed silence until then suddenly jumped up and applauded wildly. I saw it again at the ABC in Elephant and Castle, packed full of Skinheads - a new teenage phenomenon just emerging at the end of the decade - and their girls. There was none of the polite reverence of the Oxford Street audience in any part of the film, but when Ollie and Al started to peel off and prepare for the battle, the place was in uproar. Squeals of delight from the Skins' molls, mixed with disparaging remarks about the actors' organs, filled the afternoon to a backing chorus of loud hoots of derision from the bootboys all around me. Finally when we got a particularly grisly close-up of Ollie's botty, a girl to my left screamed out the classic, 'Now I remember where I've parked my bike...'. I don't know which of the two audience's reactions director Ken Russell was hoping for, but I know which was the most honest.

It was a year when it was a case of 'whatever can we do next?'.

Serge Gainsbourg and the steaming Jane Birkin managed to get three minutes of orgasmic sex to number one in the record charts with 'Je T'Aime' - then 'Private Eye' gave us their own Jane Firkin and Surge Forward.

'Hair' got everybody in a flap over its onstage nudity; we all flocked to see it, purely to assess its artistic merit you understand, and at the end of the first half members of the cast performed naked in virtual darkness for about as long as it takes a cat to get through a catflap, before their modesties were covered with a strategically placed blanket. All very permissive we didn't think...

Britain was simply becoming too hard to shock anymore. George Melly commented 'Once you've flashed your privates at the audience and shouted a few insults, there's not a lot left to do...'.

It was a bit like that with teenage rebels as well. By the end of the Sixties it seemed there was little left of the old conformities for kids to rebel against, and the shock value had gone out of wild clothes, long hair, loud music and even taking drugs.

And suddenly it was December 31st, 1969.

'Damned revolting hippies, give 'em a spell in the Army or a slap round the face with a wet fish... that'll cure 'em.'

70s

ANARCHY IN THE UK

'Honest' John James was a notorious Skinhead for a while:

> *I was sort of famous around Manchester. We used to follow United and make sure there was a bit of aggro at every game. It started as a laugh, running fights with the opposition and police, but it started to get heavy when razors and chains were being used. I packed it all in when I nearly got killed by a boot in the face.*
>
> *And I suppose I grew out of it anyway when I got into my early twenties, it was a teenage thing.*

Hell's Angels Terrify The Home Counties! More ruthless than the Rockers, more brazen than the Bikers, the California motorcycle cult that is sweeping across the suburbs!

If my memory of New Year's Eve 1959 was surprisingly clear, my memories of the chiming of midnight December 31st 1969 are distinctly vague. I seem to remember linking arms with a group of Skinheads in Trafalgar Square, and lurching and stumbling my way into another decade in a haze of Newcastle Brown Ale and a particularly vicious meat pie purchased from a stall somewhere in Soho.

I was teaching in the East End of London at the time, and the kids there showed no signs of any legacy of David Bailey, Terence Stamp or the Beatles. Their parents had remained untouched by the Summer of Love. They were in the main very poor, aggressive kids from rough homes in rough areas. They were frustrated, they were unimpressed by any authority, and they were always up for aggro.

My Honours Degree in the finer points of English Literature was of far less use to me than the sheer physical plus of being over six foot two. Far more of my lesson time was spent trying to stop a rather large Turkish boy from setting light to Thompson's hair than actually teaching them anything.

The school, like so many, was violent, it was overcrowded, truancy was quietly ignored as one way of easing the problem, and what educational standards there were were pathetically low for boys about to leave school. As one kid said to me 'Just 'cos I can't spell cat don't mean I can't kill one!'

Illiteracy was more or less the norm, and teaching methods actually seemed to encourage it. It was more important, we were forever being told, for the 'child to be able to express himself creatively than be shackled by considerations of literacy and presentation'. The fact that most of these so-called creative endeavours were illegible and incomprehensible was apparently unimportant; correcting homework was often like reading a succession of doctor's prescriptions.

Lee Parker of Tottenham, North London, encountered the last gasps of hippiedom:

> My brother and I subscribed to Melody Maker, and couldn't wait for Thursday mornings when you heard the thud of it dropping through the letter box. It was always advertising Virgin Records shops, where all the albums had large discounts, so I thought I should go down there.
>
> A friend and I walked into the shop in Oxford Street, and climbed the stairs to find ourselves in a small room packed with long-haired scruffy young men sitting round lethargically wearing headphones, listening to the latest Emerson Lake and Palmer or Average White Band. They would nod their heads slightly in time to the music. The air was thick with smoke, and the sweet sickly smell of marijuana was overwhelming.

Alcohol was the new youth drug of the Seventies. Martin Cooper recalls when you could get 'drunk for a pound and dead drunk for £1.89' in Harpenden, Herts:

> If Tom, the landlord of the Red Lion, was already half cut, a decent sized fourteen-year-old (platform soles helped) with a husky growl and a bit of bravado could get served in the roughest pub in town. With beer at 17p a pint, a couple of quid would set you up for the evening. Or you could brazen it out in the local supermarket. The check-out operators couldn't give a toss how old you were, though you might bump into a friend of the family. Well worth the risk though, when you could get a bottle of Hirondelle for £1.89 - then down to the local park to get hopelessly drunk, sing a medley of Motown hits on the way home and throw up on the extension roof before crashing out. Happy days!

Gus grew up in Fulham. Living near the Stamford Bridge football ground, he and his mates from school supported Chelsea:

We called ourselves the JNS gang - short for Junior North Stand - and we deliberately stood on the North Stand end where the away supporters were segregated. That way caused more aggravation even before things started.

There was about fifteen of us. We weren't Skinheads, the real Skinheads were all at the Shed end, but we did wear hobnail boots. We ended up getting in lumber with anyone - the Skins, then the punks when they started parading up and down the Kings Road - when they weren't being attacked by Teds that is.

No DMs, jeans and braces for us, our silver coulotte pants wafted as we punched the air and stomped our platform soles in imitation of the hero of our generation, Gary Glitter.

Some essays went on for page after rambling page without a single punctuation. One morning I decided I could stand no more, and risking insulting their intelligence I embarked on a whole lesson dedicated to 'how to use a full stop'. It could have been a disaster, but turned out to be the most successful lesson I ever taught. These kids of fourteen and fifteen sat squeezed into undersized desks spellbound as someone actually showed them on the blackboard how to put a big round dot when they'd got to the end of a sentence and a big capital letter when they began the next one.

For the only time in my mercifully brief teaching career, you could hear a pin drop. I think it was the first time in their lives anyone had ever bothered to explain it to them. (Full stop)

A Bit of Bovver

(Capital letter) Most of the kids in the school and that whole area of south-east London were Skinheads. With shaven heads, upturned jeans and big Doctor Marten 'bovver' boots, they roamed the streets of New Cross, Deptford and Lewisham at night in large sprawling gangs looking for 'aggro'. They kept in large numbers for safety, and attacked anyone and everyone coming the other way who wasn't a Skin. They gay bashed, they Paki bashed, and they pulled the wings off hippies.

And of course at weekends, the best aggro of all was at football matches. In the early Seventies trouble on the terraces was a new but depressingly regular feature at football grounds, and many grown men stopped going altogether - or at least didn't take their kids with them. I remember going to one match at a well-known ground in the Midlands where, amongst a large haul of weapons taken off the boot-boys before the match, the police found a flame-thrower and two cross bows!

The Skinheads were the first teenage sub-group not to have specific idols or role models in pop music - though they did latch on to elements of punk and such later in the decade - and this unwelcome 'loyalty' to certain football clubs seemed to take its place.

The Skins felt that such violence was the only outlet for them in a society that believed it was great to be young in post-Sixties Britain. For a few it probably was....for a massive majority it clearly wasn't.

MOULDY OLD DOUGH

Music in the early years of the Seventies was as confused as the kids. So many influences had hit us between the eyes since the mid Sixties that we seemed to be ripe for anything...or maybe just punch drunk from too much.

The Beatles had disbanded, Jim Morrison, Jimi Hendrix and Janis Joplin were dead. Fossilising figures such as the Stones and Paul McCartney were still being wheeled out on interminable tours, but they and their fans certainly weren't teenagers anymore.

The opening years of the decade brought a wide range of 'mature' music to the charts which included Black Sabbath, Led Zepplin - both of whom heralded heavy metal, with its audiences of post-hippy longhairs frantically miming with cardboard guitars - the cuddly Carpenters, and number ones from George 'Hari Krishna' Harrison, Benny Hill, Clive Dunn (with 'Grandad'), and the extraordinary 'Mouldy Old Dough' from Lieutenant Pigeon, who included someone's granny on the piano! To teenagers it was becoming increasingly apparent that pop music was dominated by 'boring old farts'.

Oi! We've got bands as well - Last Resort, Cockney Rejects, and not forgetting the Four Skins - apart from that, we're just interested in sole music.

Aggrophobia: 'Skinhead loyalty to certain football clubs and far right groups like the British National Party is acted out in a ritual of violence'

Social study report, early Seventies.

TROUBLE'N'STRIFE

1970 ushered in a decade of industrial unrest. The new Conservative Government and Unions were locked in bitter confrontation, and unemployment rose to nearly a million, the highest since the Thirties. The boom was over. In America, Nixon was desperately trying to get the country out of Vietnam, as a vote catcher as much as for any higher motive, yet still the body bags came home. Marshall McLuhan, the media guru, said 'Television brought the brutality of war into the comfort of the living room. Vietnam was lost in the living rooms of America, not on the battlefields of Vietnam...'. It was a war that no one any longer had any faith in, or any clue as to why they were fighting. And the same year, rioting students were shot dead by the National Guard at Ohio's Kent State University.

Things were certainly taking a turn for the worse after the optimism and euphoria of the past few years, but there were indications that one or two of the freedoms of the Sixties were achieving something. The law on divorce was widened to include a Breakdown of Marriage that did not necessarily end in adultery or violence. Feminism and women's rights were issues that dominated the decade. For the first time missiles were thrown at the Miss World contest, right in the middle of a rivetting interview with a girl who wanted to 'travel the world, meet people and do lots of charity work involving animals'.

Who remembers monkey boots? Janet Valentine does:

They were hideous brown leather walking boots with heavy tread and yellow laces, which made my dainty size four feet look at least two sizes larger.

'We're for the Union Jack, but that doesn't make us all National Front. For us it's just natural to be patriotic.'

Political protest was Mary Jackson's act of rebellion in the early Seventies:

It was 1971 and I went to the dentist. As I lay recumbent in his chair, he glanced down at my desert boots and remarked 'Those must be your marching boots !'. He was right. My left boot had a badly drawn Anti-Apartheid symbol on it, and the right sported the Ban the Bomb sign in blue biro. We were always going on demonstrations for one thing and another - South Africa or the Trade Unions. They would start at Speaker's Corner and finish at Trafalgar Square, where speakers would entertain the assembly.

We usually found a discarded placard that we carried with pride, and soon learnt whatever the chant for that day was. As we marched down Oxford Street, one of our friends saw some old shop dummies outside a department store. She picked them up and each of us held a limb, or a torso, or head. We thought that this was terribly funny and Monty Python-ish, but somehow we always got the surrealist humour slightly wrong.

VAN ROUGH

About this time I was living in my Mini van. After a particularly heated row with my then girlfriend I roared off into the night leaving our Fulham flat behind, only to realise after I'd cooled down at about three in the morning that I had nowhere to go. Stubborn as ever I slept the night in the van, then the next, and the next, and found that I rather liked it. It was quite cosy, cheap and handy for school as I used to park right outside.

The kids from school would wake me by hammering on the windscreen in the morning, then it'd be a quick shower and coffee and toast in the staffroom before another day battling with the Full Stop and the Skinheads. My proudest moment for years was when there was a tap on the window one morning and the postman brought me my first two letters, addressed C.J. Tarrant, 161 GLO (Grey Van), Sprules Road, London SE4.

The biggest drawback to the joys of living in my Mini van was my love life. The van was quite well appointed with carpeting and cushions, and ladies could even get used to the idea of having a late cup of coffee from a calor gas burner between their knees, but when they said (sadly all too infrequently) 'Shall we go back to your place?' to be told 'Well...actually we're in it', somehow it nearly always put them off.

LAMBTONGATE

Around the end of 1972 some not particularly significant burglars were caught breaking into a not particularly significant place in Washington called Watergate, but it didn't hit the headlines immediately.

What did make the front pages over the next few months was good old Lord Lambton who resigned as all good honest Ministers do when he was found to have had an ongoing relationship with a call girl called Norma Levy. Just like the Profumo case years before, the press had a field day. Whips, masks, manacles, suits of armour, cream buns, it had all been there for Lambton's quiet afternoons with Norma. As the woman in our local paper shop said, 'It's always sex with the Tories and money fiddles with the Labour lot'. At the time we all wondered what it would ever be with the Liberals, but the Thorpe trial was going to reach new heights of tabloid tackiness in the years ahead.

If British politicians knew when the game was up and did the decent thing, Richard Nixon in the States believed in nothing of the sort. As the Watergate scandal broke Tricky Dicky just kept hanging on in the White House like a limpet on a luxury liner. It was easier for us this side of the Great Pond to see how he was obviously involved in the whole business, yet every night the news would quote yet another American opinion poll reaffirming the naive belief that their President would never lie to them.

ROLLER OVER BEETHOVEN

The rest of British newspaper space at this time was given over to the under thirteens - the teenyboppers who were sobbing and squealing their way on to front pages everywhere, and Mums and Dads blamed the telly. It started back in the Sixties with the Monkees, and now there were two American TV imports that had girlie audiences glued to the gogglebox. The Osmonds - the Brothers Grin as they were known to an ever-grateful toothpaste industry - with the gleaming white Donny, the wholesome Marie and the unspeakable Little Jimmy, vying for pubescent popularity with the Partridge Family and the dashing David Cassidy.

We've had the mini skirt and the maxi, now the latest fashion fad is hot pants - with leatherette stack-heel boots, just the thing for easy riders like Suzy from Streatham, seen here with biker boyfriend Jim. Lucky Jim!

Eventually David announced - shock, horror, squeal - that he was breaking away from the squeaky clean Partridge clan. 'I'm going to be David Cassidy from now on' he told a hushed teenybop world, 'I am no longer going to be Keith Partridge'. And who could blame him? When he finally came to Britain 500 little girls cried their eyes out when he didn't arrive at Manchester as scheduled, but snuck in via Luton of all places. An emaciated Susan Gaskell, 14, from Staffordshire, said tearfully she'd been saving her dinner money for three months to get to Manchester on 'D for David Day', and then he never showed. His UK tour was one non-stop squeal as Alsatians were used to keep the teenyboppers back from the ex-Mr Partridge.

I remember going to see him in the Midlands in concert. And I'm ever so sorry David - or is it Keith? - but in spite of all the hysteria around me I actually fell fast asleep. In fairness it was possibly the twelve or so beers I'd drunk before the concert but then again if I hadn't been completely out of my brain I'd certainly never have bought a ticket in the first place.

Home-grown heroes for the teenies were led by ex-hippy 'bopping elf' Marc Bolan with T-Rex, and Slade - who despite having discarded a Skinhead image fairly quickly, retained a yobbish illiteracy in their song titles ('Coz I Luv You', 'Take Me Bak Ome' etc). Slade's Noddy Holder was actually charged with obscenity after saying 'What a load of XXXX' at a live concert in Glasgow.

The onslaught of Bubblegum music sees the average age of pop fans plummet as nursery-rhyme rock takes over the singles charts, the Sweet's 'Wig Wam Bam' rivalled only by Suzi Quatro's 'Can The Can'.

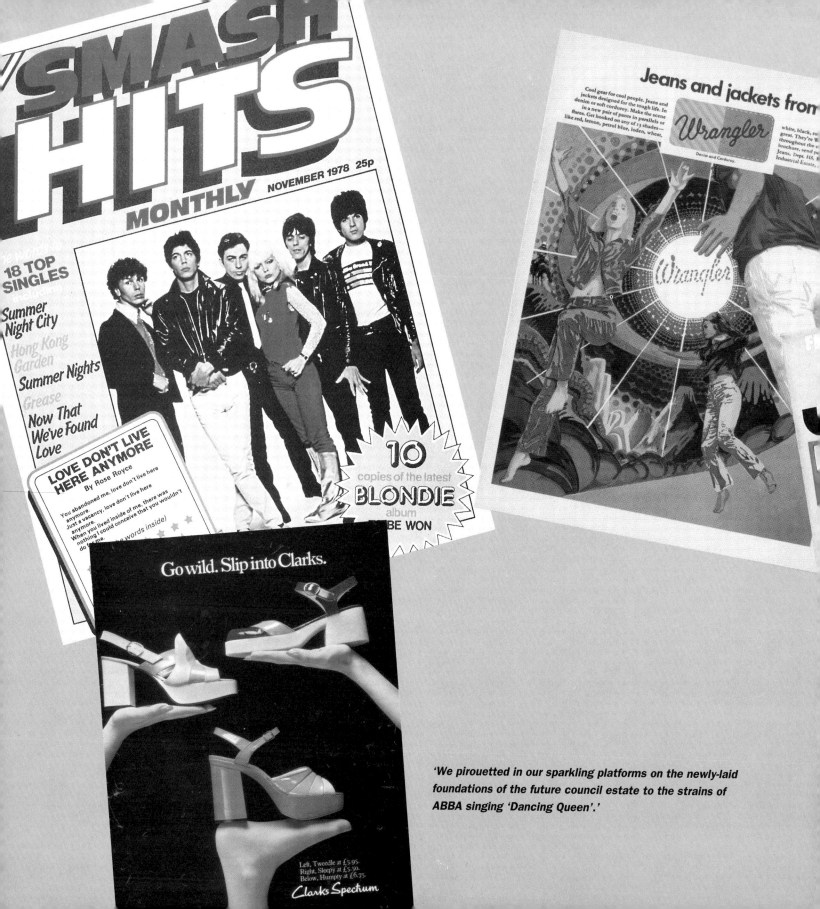

SMASH HITS MONTHLY

NOVEMBER 1978 25p

18 TOP SINGLES

including

Summer Night City
Hong Kong Garden
Summer Nights
Grease
Now That We've Found Love

LOVE DON'T LIVE HERE ANYMORE
By Rose Royce

You abandoned me, love don't live here anymore.
Just a vacancy, love don't live here anymore.
When you lived inside of me, there was nothing I could conceive that you wouldn't do for me.

(full words inside)

10 copies of the latest BLONDIE album TO BE WON

'We pirouetted in our sparkling platforms on the newly-laid foundations of the future council estate to the strains of ABBA singing 'Dancing Queen'.'

'Disco arrived with two movies, 'Car Wash' and 'Saturday Night Fever'. What must we have looked like marching four abreast clapping out the rhythm of the 'Car Wash' theme, not to mention the lads trying - and failing - to copy John Travolta's strut.'

Sharon Butler was a typical teenybopper:

I don't know how my mother put up with me, it must have been absolutely impossible. When the Osmonds came I queued overnight to get a ticket, and told her I was staying at my mate's. Of course, my friend had told her Mum the same, and we were both caught out. They wouldn't believe we'd been queueing, they were sure we'd been with some lads or at an all-night party, till they saw the pictures of the queues in the paper. Then it was David Essex. I tried to sneak into his hotel when he came to Birmingham, I was only fifteen, got thrown out on my ear - literally - by the doorman. This time my Mum thought I'd been in a fight!

Rollers Rool, OK. They call us the Tartan Terrors, just because we'll do anything to get near Les, Derek, Alan, Woody and Eric.

Dubbed 'Glam rock', pop seemed to involve a lot of body-hugging costumes, mascara and glitter and camping about, taken to its extreme by David Bowie at one level and Gary Glitter at the other....who was sending up who was often hard to tell.

Gary Glitter probably did more for sales of the chest wig than any other figure in the history of modern music. His show was pure self parody, and again there were riots across the UK every time he achieved the impossible and once again squeezed himself into his barely fitting gold lurex hot pants.

The 'Glam' period was responsible for some of the worst excesses in rock fashion, a genre not given to sartorial subtlety at the best of times, most memorable of which were probably the spangled six-inch thick platform soles worn by the likes of Marc Bolan, Elton John and other total exhibitionists.

But the biggest and best riots were by fans of the Bay City Rollers. The young Scottish band took the teeny population by storm with a string of hits such as 'Shang A Lang' and 'Bye Bye Baby', and scenes of total hysteria erupted wherever they appeared. There were many injured and always a number of arrests, but the biggest problem the authorities had with Rollers fans, who aped their acned heroes with tartan scarves and baggy trousers that finished a good two inches above the ankle, was that they were so young it was almost impossible to know how to deal with them.

I remember trying to film the Rollers arriving at a concert in the Midlands. The whole of central Birmingham was sealed off, and the streets were lined with police in riot gear. I interviewed one burly Brummy copper with his helmet missing and a sobbing deranged ten-year-old girl under each arm, both screaming four-letter words at him. 'Trouble is' he said, 'now I've caught them, what the hell do I do with them?'.

As teenyboppers gave way to the even teenier weenyboppers, parents refused point blank to let their offspring go and see the Rollers for their own safety, angry tantrums erupting in thousands of homes.

The only other serious rioting I saw around the same time was among old age pensioners outside Birmingham Cathedral. Just how far televison could scramble the nation's mind was clear when Meg Richardson married the oily Hugh Mortimer on 'Crossroads', a confusingly popular soap opera.

The presents from the public were bizarre enough, including three piece suites, colour tellies and electric cookers, but what was really terrifying was the shouting and fighting among the couple of thousand little old ladies massed outside the Cathedral, convinced the whole thing was for real.

One deranged granny grabbed me by the shirt and sobbed 'Chris, Chris, he's all wrong for Meg, yow've got to stop eet....'

All very worrying.

LOONS AND LOONEYS

Like the Rollers fans, our dress was our uniform. There were Rockers and Glam Rockers, there were Skins and lounging around dusty jukeboxes in outlying corners of the provinces there were cells of ageing Teds. Some of us were still even hippies with Afro-inspired hairstyles, headbands and floor-length kaftans. In fact the cheesecloth-loons-and-clogs look was very much a left-

'Keep Britain Tidy', a slogan for the Seventies in streets littered with uncollected rubbish and swooning teenies.

over from the late Sixties that came into its own in the early Seventies. And wearing the wrong uniform in the wrong part of town at the wrong time of night was still a sure way of getting a damn good kicking....

I certainly had no intention of giving up my Afghan coat even though I'd moved from my elegant south-east London Mini van to the rather silly and unimportant world of television with the Midlands regional News At Six. I'd interview anyone from politicians to old ladies who'd lost their budgies, the latter usually proving more interesting than the former. But what I did like was a good looney - and every day ATV would wheel one in and I'd interview them. I did 'em all, from the upside-down beer drinkers to the world's greatest soot juggler. And for a while I was very very happy.

Industrial gloom brought with it strikes, power cuts and the three-day week to conserve energy. By the middle of the decade unemployment had risen to over two million. Labour got back into power and settled with the striking miners by giving coalface workers the princely sum of £45 a week. This went a long way in an England where a bottle of gin cost £2.50 pence and the price of petrol was up to over fifty pence per gallon.

I lived in Lambeth for a while next door to a really nice guy called Lenny the Burglar, and whenever I'd lost my keys, which was most of the time, Lenny would disappear furtively up his own rear drainpipe and emerge triumphant and grinning from inside my front door.

Princess Anne and husband Captain Mark Phillips were shot at in their car outside Buckingham Palace, and although neither of them were hurt examination showed one bullet had passed very close between them and gone through the seat.

Ringo Starr and Keith Moon were thrown out of the Playboy Club for having a 'bit of a rave-up', Joe Cocker was charged with drug offences in the middle of an Australian tour, and Moon 'The Loon' was banned from most American hotel chains for throwing chairs and settees out of windows, often with people still sitting on them. Blue-collar rock found a new hero in Bruce Springsteen, while Rod Stewart went solo, Ronnie Wood joined the Stones, and Elton John moved into an English mansion whispered to have cost over £50,000! Well, he needed somewhere to keep those towering shoes and his collection of outsize specs. The Who may have gone mainstream by producing their rock opera 'Tommy' as a movie, but as ever they were still keen to prove how tough they were - Roger Daltrey said of one incident 'Pete was being held back by two roadies, he was spitting at me and hitting me with his guitar...I was forced to lay one on him...'.

The singles chart was dominated by people like Sweet, Mud with 'Lonely This Christmas' - so they should be, - the New Seekers, The Carpenters and Paper Lace (remember 'Billy Don't Be A Hero?'). Cliff Richard had sadly failed to crack the Eurovision Song Contest in '73 with 'Congratulations', though frankly we were all puzzled that anybody would really want to win the dreadful thing, and the following year it was won by an unknown Swedish outfit called ABBA. They chose their name from the initials of the members, Agnetha, Benny, Bjorn and Anni-Frid, but I always wondered if they'd have done the same thing had their names been Benny, Ursula, Manfred and Sonja. Probably not....

In London the BBC had promised new breezy fun programmes to counter the threat of Capital Radio and LBC, Britain's first two commercial radio stations that opened in October '74. We're still waiting for them to fulfill the promise....

David Harris got off on glam rock:

Music during the Seventies was pretty boring for me until the arrival of Gary Glitter and Slade. I loved the music and clothes. Coloured hair was part of the image and we used food colouring to turn our hair red or green. I went out in the rain once and ruined a new white shirt.

Con-man or chameleon? Marc Bolan moved from Mod to Hippy to Glam with ease. Not so easy for the rest of us, sneaking into sisters' bedrooms to 'borrow' lipstick and eyeshadow.

Angie Wilson recalls the Summer Of '76, just before punk took everybody by surprise:

> *The summer of 1976 was one of the hottest on record. I will always remember it from seeing the Stones at Knebworth. They played to about 200,000 people. The stage took the form of a large pair of lips, and took so long to inflate that the Stones came on three hours late. They played all their old hits, and Jagger kept saying 'What's next, Keef ?' between songs.*

Carry On Camping: the macho men of music are swept aside with a flick of the wrist to make way for names like Glitter, Stardust, Sweet and Queen.

I finally managed to turn my own gibbering lunacy into a full-time career, when the company I worked for, ATV, started TISWAS, a low budget Saturday morning kids' show that was scheduled for two weeks but eventually took over seven years of my life. It closed Saturday morning pictures all over the country, and was even nominated for a BAFTA award. It was anarchic, it was irreverent, and kids of all ages loved it.

RASTAMAN VIBRATIONS

In 1976 we sweltered in the hottest summer since records began, and suffered the worst drought for a quarter of a century. Car washes, hoses and garden sprinklers were all banned, and in the hot weather tempers frayed. The traditional Notting Hill Carnival had always been a happy-go-lucky occasion, but this year for the first time it was marred by violence, drug busts and running battles with the police.

Tension with the police had been building up over recent years as a new generation of young blacks born in Britain found they had even less chance of money and a job than their white counterparts. They were regularly hassled and searched by officers of the law, and were convinced that it was purely on the basis of the colour of their skin - and sadly in many cases they were right.

GOB ONLY KNOWS

The second half of 1976 also saw the explosion of punk rock. Groups like The Sex Pistols, The Damned and The Clash challenged the whole complacency that the rock music scene had fallen into. Their sound was raw, it was accused of being musically inept and incited riots. Most established rock stars hated everything to do with it but it kicked the Rock Star syndrome up the botty, at least for a couple of years.

At the beginning of the year the Pistols' manager Malcolm McLaren had said 'I'm going to change the face of the music scene', and to a certain extent he did. He went on 'All the music at the moment is by and for thirty-year-old hippies. Boring. The Sex Pistols are fresh and young. They are kids playing music for the kids. Not some property tycoon singing 'My Generation'. They're from the streets and the dole queues, they're representative of most of the kids of this country'.

They attracted violence and actually thrived on it. They wanted to make an impact any way they knew how, they wanted to be somebody, just for a brief while.

The punks - not just the bands, but the thousands of kids at street level who identified with them - showed a total disregard for everything. Their hairstyles were often home-done creations with great tufts cut out, or huge cockerel crests sticking out of an otherwise completely shaved head. They wore safety pins in their ears, and studs in their nostrils. Their clothes were grubby vests, T-shirts with carefully cut holes all over them, black bin bags, moth-eaten black stockings, bondage gear and ripped jeans. Like the Skinheads before them, they wore boots for aggro.

'...and you're not spending a nice sunny Saturday morning stuck in front of the television watching that ridiculous TISWAS. You could be taking Jeannie to the park, or helping me with the shopping, or meeting your mates in the pub...'. Such despairing cries were soon to be heard from wives and mothers the length and breadth of the land.

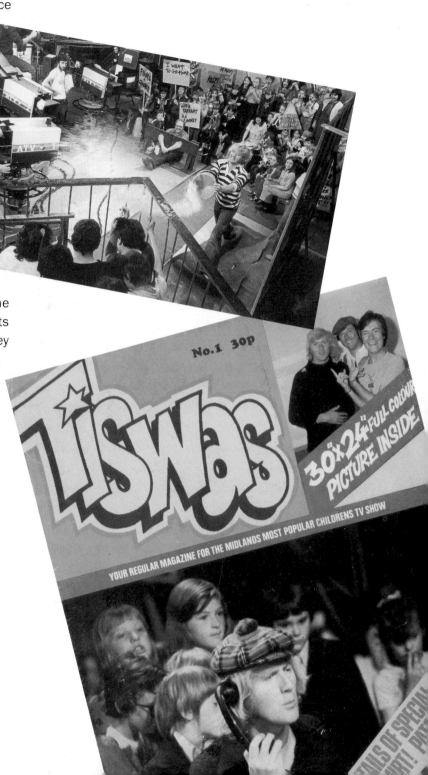

Even their names shouted aggression - Siouxsie and the Banshees, The Boomtown Rats, The Vibrators, The Stranglers, The Slits, Slaughter and the Dogs, Snatch and Penetration. They contrasted sharply with everybody else on the music scene, and that was the whole point.

Meanwhile the charts at the time were a strange combination of Wings, the Bay City Rollers, Abba and a Disco Duck that desperately needed stuffing. So there was some room for fresh air - or even a bit of a pong - and just maybe Johnny Rotten and co could provide it.

Commercialism as always wasn't far away. EMI raced in and signed the Sex Pistols in the fastest record deal ever, the group getting an advance of £40,000. Within three months they were sacked by the company as being more trouble than they were worth. They were then snapped up by A&M Records who in turn sacked them inside seven days for drunkenly rampaging around the company office. One company employee at the time said 'I'm amazed they lasted so long'. The Pistols did somehow manage to make a great deal of money in a very short space of time without actually releasing a record.

Their most famous outrage was when they appeared live on Bill Grundy's early evening TV show, and treated Bill to what the press called 'the filthiest language ever heard on British television'. Horrified women packers at EMI refused to handle their single, 'Anarchy in the UK', which made sales difficult to say the least. One lorry driver was so incensed by their effing and blinding that he kicked his television screen in. He said he was 'so disgusted and angry I took a swing with my *!?*ing boot', blowing up the set and nearly killing himself in the process. But overall, the publicity did the Pistols no harm at all - and mainman Malcy, if not his punkaloid protégés, certainly knew it.

Jamie Banks experienced the horror of punk hairdos going wrong:

> *Some mates of mine organised a kind of punk festival over a Saturday afternoon and evening in July '78. It was just local bands thrashing away on naff guitars and dodgy drum kits. I spiked my hair with a mixture of sugar and water, it worked really well and I really looked the part, pretty outrageous I thought. However, I didn't take into account that it was a warm summer's day. My head turned into a huge sticky mess and nobody would come near me because I was surrounded by a massive swarm of flies.*

Phew, What A Scorcher! Tabloids in surprise crusade against Rotten language.

As The Sex Pistols, The Clash and The Damned prepared for a nationwide tour, McLaren said, 'There may well be violence at some of the gigs because it's violent music. We don't necessarily think violence is a bad thing'. There was a lot of violence and a lot of cancellations from terrified promoters. They didn't just rip up the cinema seats like the rock'n'roll fans of the Fifties, they tore the place to shreds.

It was Virgin who eventually bailed out the Pistols, with their third contract, and this time they actually managed to get a record in the shops. It was 'God Save The Queen', released to coincide with Queen Elizabeth's Silver Jubilee in 1977. No TV company would carry adverts for it, hardly any radio station would play it, and so it went straight to Number One.

Once again teenagers had someone they could look down to.

Pogo Fever

After a 1978 tour of the US the Sex Pistols fell apart. Johnny Rotten was sacked by McLaren and sent home from the States with a smacked wrist, Paul Cook and Steve Jones made a video with balding train robber Ronnie Biggs, for reasons nobody ever seemed to have comprehended. The tour was a disaster, and a few months later Sid Vicious died of a heroin overdose while on parole for the fatal stabbing of his girlfriend Nancy Spungen. Rotten remained as quotable as ever when he summed up love as 'two minutes and fifty seconds of squelching noises'.

But if the Pistols had come and gone faster than Simon Dee or even Crispian St Peters, some of the other New Wave bands finally gained acceptance across the world, and surprisingly punk eventually did rather better in America than over here. The hottest US punk properties were Talking Heads, The Ramones and Debbie Harry with Blondie.

'...groups like Johnny's help Society by bringing kids in off the street. A friend of ours thinks the Pistols are doing more good for the country than James Callaghan...'
Johnny Rotten's mother, Islington Gazette, May 1977

The delectable Deborah was a cult obsession some time before she became a fully fledged pop icon. I remember a close mate of mine, a big blonde guy from Sheffield with a permanent five o'clock shadow, went through a very odd 'Wow, don't I look like Debbie Harry' period. All very disturbing for those of us who shared a flat with him. It was about three months before his arrest for sheep worrying.

Initially plagued by fighting at their gigs, The Clash finally got themselves together. Generation X actually admitted they'd 'quite like to be stars really' and charismatic lead singer of the Boomtown Rats, Bob Geldof, said what he did was 'A job. No big deal. But rock'n'roll along with TV and the movies is a great twentieth century art form....'

If it did nothing else, punk rock gave me a chance to master yet another dance step to add to my minimal repetoire. The Pogo was the dance for people who couldn't dance at all; basically you just jumped up in the air as high as you could with your arms at your sides, and if you could bump against somebody else on the way up and spit - 'gob' was the punks' elegant term - at somebody on the way down, then even better. It's still one of my best steps at High Society occasions and May Balls, although bafflingly girlfriends tend to make their excuses and go back and sit down.

Barry Parkin let fly as one of The Zips:

I was in a punk band in college called The Zips. We bought our instruments from Woolworths and learnt to play in a fortnight. It was just a loud noise really. We disrupted the 'O' level exams at the nearby Grammar School by making too much noise.

135

Half a tube of the old EVO Stick up yer nose really makes yer 'air stand on end.

Ricky Jones was in on the punk explosion in Liverpool:

A club called Eric's was opened by a big guy called Roger Eagle, just down the road from where the Cavern had been in the Sixties. The first local band to make it down there was Deaf School, a gang of art students, just before punk started. Then the New Wave groups arrived, and Eric's was the centre of a new scene.

I remember showing Debbie Harry the way there from Lime Street Station. Blondie had come up for a gig on the train!

The other great meeting place was Probe Records just around the corner from Eric's. On a Saturday you couldn't move in there for every imaginable style of punk, it was like a youth club. What made us laugh was the London punks moaning about being unemployed - it had never seemed much different in Liverpool, only now the place seemed to have got a lot grottier.

Pamela Boyd's headmaster tried to get in on the act:

...he dyed his hair from white to black over the summer holiday. When we came back to school with green hair, he was too embarrassed to say anything.

In total contrast to anything remotely punk, the smash hits of 1977 were 'Saturday Night Fever' by the Bee Gees, and John Travolta in the movie 'Grease'. Travolta never pogoed once.

Jovial Jim Callaghan took over as Prime Minister from Harold Wilson, otherwise it was business as usual; even Britain's undertakers went on strike, with 800 bodies remaining unburied while their pay demand was sorted out. Nobody dared die.

MAGGIE'S FARM

Kids had their suspicions of the Establishment's stupidity reaffirmed in 1978 when Parliament allowed itself to be broadcast live on the radio. Our chosen representatives behaved like squabbling schoolkids - worse than squabbling schoolkids some would argue. Within days people were complaining that the House of Commons was becoming a laughing stock because it sounded no better than a farmyard. Minister William Price said 'The great majority of listeners are appalled by the bellowing, abuse, baying, hee hawing and the rest. We have a public relations disaster on our hands. The nation can't take this shock. We really must behave...'. They're still trying.

Meanwhile inside and outside the corridors of power, women continued to flex their muscles.

Still a bit of a teenager after all these years Princess Margaret was finally allowed by her big sister the Queen to leave Lord Snowdon and was spotted on the Isle of Mustique with a posh hippy gardener called Roddy Llewelyn, while Anna Ford became ITN's first female news reader - and we all agreed she had a much nicer nose than Alastair Burnett.

Of less obvious attraction was Mrs Thatcher, known to schoolkids everywhere as 'the milk snatcher', who was now firmly established as the terrifying leader of the

Opposition, with an even more alarming possibility that she might get into No 10 Downing Street before too long.

With her nicely ironed hair and a voice that could cut through a coal face, Margaret Hilda Thatcher became Prime Minister in May 1979. A newspaper at the time ran a less than flattering cartoon of her in full battle attire with the caption 'The Most Frightening Man On Earth'. Her opening speech was typical of Thatcher things to come - 'Look, I beat four chaps and that's all, now let's get down to some work.'

THE GUNGE FACTOR

By the end of the decade TISWAS had gone national, and was the hottest new cult TV show in London. We'd been doing the show for six years with hardly a complaint, now suddenly every social worker and child psychologist was demanding we be thrown off the airwaves.

TISWAS was certainly as chaotic as it looked. Every week we would pack the studio with a mixture of (in order of importance) baying kids, animals and pop stars. It was live, it was under-rehearsed and it was sometimes utter drivel, but there was an energy and an inventiveness about it all that when it worked was one of the most satisfying things I could imagine.

I once spent a whole morning rolling about in custard with Annie Lennox and Sheena Easton. And if you think I enjoyed it, how very right you'd be. What exactly was the reason for it? Who the hell cares? What made it different from other kids programmes, like the squeaky clean Noel Edmonds' 'Swop Shop' on the other side was its huge teen and adult audience. From what started as a little Saturday morning kiddie's show, the anarchic giant that it became found that more than half its audience were over eighteen.

Dave Redmond recalls the enthusiasm of punk:

We were all working class and proud of it, except that we weren't actually working 'cos there was no work to be had. Except lousy jobs that nobody wanted, monotonous jobs.

Punk gave us something that had been missing, for our own age group - the rock stars were for punters in their twenties and thirties, we called them Boring Old Farts or worse.

It didn't matter that the bands couldn't play properly half the time... it meant we could almost do the same ourselves if we could be bothered.

Down the Roxy...Siouxsie and the Banshees, Penetration...a few Carlsberg Specials, pogo off your head...gob over the band, puke up in the street...then the last train home to Bromley.

'Punk's all about recycling the past with the do-it-yourself look of today.'

We filled a cage with grown-ups every week and let the kids in the studio pelt them with rubbish. Women would arrive for the ordeal in their best clothes with hair done specially, only to be covered in buckets of gunge and gallons of water seconds after going on the air. There was a nine-month waiting list for the cage, and we sometimes had theme cages - taxmen, policemen, headmasters, even a cage full of vicars!

We were even briefly pop stars. As the Four Bucketeers, Sally James, Bob Cargolees, John Gorman (formerly of the Scaffold) and myself had a hit with 'The Bucket Of Water Song'. In spite of absolutely no plays on the BBC, it sold so well they had to let us appear on Top Of The Pops. With the huge audiences TISWAS brought to ITV every Saturday morning, we were very much the enemy, and to say we weren't made welcome at Wood Lane would be an understatement...which other guest group didn't have a dressing room and was asked to go out and change in their car...?

PUNKS TO PORSCHES

When they weren't watching TISWAS, the teenyboppers had found a new hero at the end of ten years of more or less non-stop squealing, and one more likely to survive the test of time - Sting and his group Police. Sting was as surprised by the adolescent adulation as anybody, but actually admitted that he rather enjoyed it. 'To a lot of people teenyboppers are a sub-species not even to be entertained. I don't agree. If you can transcend the screaming you can take a generation with you into something else. It's a real challenge.' Certainly a speech most unlikely to be uttered by a Bay City Roller or Little Jimmy Osmond.

Despite all the traumas surrounding the rise and fall of the Sex Pistols, the acceptable face of punk was now mainstream pop. The Clash forced CBS to sell their 'London Calling' album at a reduced rate by taking a lower royalty - 'I want to reach the kids in school' said Joe Strummer.

The punks may have shaken things up a bit, but for all the aggro and wild publicity, their actual musical legacy was quite small, and disturb the Music Establishment and 'property developer rock stars' they hardly did at all.

Even as a focus for rebellious youth, they became a bit of a cliché. The biggest selling picture postcard sent from London, outselling even those of Buckingham Palace, is the one showing the punk with a bright red cockerel-pointed Mohican hairstyle; rebel youth reduced to the role of tourist trivia.

Bob Geldof encouraged truancy with 'I Don't Like Mondays', and it was ageing hippies Pink Floyd who had the last hit of the Seventies with 'Another Brick In The Wall'.....'We don't need no education, we don't need no thought control.....Teacher, leave the kids alone...'. The Thatcher years were to have a tremendous influence on young people. She presided over a new section of the population who wanted the material things in life, and wanted to show them off, the Yuppies. They were an Eighties phenomenon of course, but the signs were there at the end of the Seventies when the bleeper was first introduced for young people in a hurry, to be followed by all the posers hardware, from mobile phone to in-car fax machine and jacuzzi!

The reign of the Iron Lady heralded a boom in silk suits with unpronounceable Italian labels inside, matt black Designer everything, gelled hair, the rocketing property market, and the yoyoing stock market. In fact the Yuppies represented exactly what young people had previously rebelled against - and which no doubt their kids would eventually reject, if they found time to have any.

'My dad was trying to make polite conversation with my friend Jake. They couldn't have looked more different, my dad in his jacket and tie and Jake with his jeans in shreds, bits of leather and chains draped around him and bright green vertical hair. My dad didn't dare ask him to sit down in case the green rubbed off on the sofa.'

Punk was a big city craze in many ways, as Allan Robertson recalls:

> *Punk never really took off in South Devon. One of the boys at college had blue hair, but that was about it. Being by the coast, we wore shorts and bright coloured T-shirts. I wore a safety pin through my Hawaiian shirt once.*

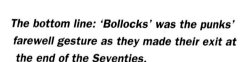

'PEOPLE TRY TO PUT US DOWN...'

What rebellion there was had hardened in the Seventies. There was none of the euphoria of the mid Sixties, it was an altogether more aggressive decade; 'Clockwork Orange', 'The Godfather', Stiff Records... There was outrage over Chuck Berry's Ding a Ling and the Boomtown Rats giving away live rats on stage.

It had been the decade of Mick McGahey and Red Robbo; the Balcombe Street Siege, Janie Jones, 'George Davis Is Innocent' and streakers everywhere. It was hard for mere teenagers to be anything more than a little bit menacing in an era that gave us Black September, the Baader-Meinhof gang, the Jackal, the Yorkshire Ripper, the Black Panther, Son of Sam and Idi Amin.

Not to mention the kidnap of little rich girl Patty Hearst, the return of the ear of Paul Getty III, and the banning of Big Ears and Noddy for being rabid racists. But the wheel would never turn full circle, and it was a mercifully long long way from Johnnie Ray's 'Little White Cloud That Cried', Tommy Steele's 'Little White Bull' and Jimmy Young's 'Man From Laramie'. The teen genie had been let loose on the world for three decades, and things would never be the same again....

The bottom line: 'Bollocks' was the punks' farewell gesture as they made their exit at the end of the Seventies.

Jodie Andrews tried a little bit of everything:

I suppose the worst thing we got involved in was glue sniffing. It got a bit of a craze for a while at school. Some of the kids there managed to get their hands on dope, smoking it in the playground in front of the teachers! But for the rest of us, it was cans of strong lager and glue.

We were Gothic punks - black, black, black everything - and eye make-up like a horror film. It was Siouxie And The Banshees meet The Damned. We looked like zombies. And when we'd been sniffing, we felt like zombies.

It was so stupid, through a plastic bag....you'd vomit after a while, or just pass out. I think we did it because there was no other way to get out of it....I'd come home and just stare at my Dad watching the telly. The papers called us the Blank Generation, and that's what we were - bored stiff.

For Mark Davies-Markham it was alcohol that sent him wild, when he and his mates went to see Dr Feelgood at Liverpool Stadium:

First time we'd had a proper drinking session, a lethal mix of Dry Martini and Cream Soda....we kept rocking on the row of seats, until we all fell back on to the row behind and knocked everyone down like dominoes. The bouncers waded in, and we scattered. Next day at school I was terrified...what if they tracked us down, did us for vandalism. From behind the Echo at tea my Dad coughed and sniffed, then laid the paper out for me to see - CRAZY POP FANS CAUSE HAVOC was the headline above a picture of our row of wrecked seats. 'I bet those yobbos were on drugs lad...'. I gulped and nearly choked on my last spaghetti hoop - 'Dry Martini and Cream Soda'. He wasn't listening.

ACKNOWLEDGEMENTS

Sian Facer **Editor**

Nick Thompson **Production**

The Publishers would like to thank the following organisations for their kind permission to reproduce the photographs in this book:-

The Advertising Archive 114, 124 top right, 125 bottom left; Aquarius Picture Library 15 inset; The BBC Photo Library 39, 55 right, 59 centre and bottom, 62 top, /Harry Goodwin 75; The British Film Institute 46, 55 right, 71; Camera Press 106-107, 143, /Simon Archer 136-137, /Terry Smith 115 bottom, 118 top, /Homer Sykes 116-7, /Gavin Watson 119; The Design Museum 22 centre, 38, 41 top, 76 bottom, 118 bottom, 130 left, 133, 140 top, /by courtesy of EMI records 37 inset, 63 right, /Smash Hits 124 top left; John Frost Historical Newspapers 61 bottom; The Ronald Grant Archive 43 top, 44 bottom inset; The Hulton Picture Company 10, 17, 18-19, 21, 25 top and bottom, 26-27, 33 top and bottom, 36 bottom, 37 cut-out, 40 bottom, 42 top, 44-45, 47, 48, 57, 65 inset, 76 top, 82, 88-89, 90, 94 bottom, 104, 115 top, 120, 121, 127 top, 137 inset, 140 bottom, 142; The Kobal Collection 42 bottom, 44 top inset; London Features International 129, 134; Monty Python 109; Robert Opie 14 inset, 16 inset, 22 left and right, 23, 40 top right, 41 centre, 50 left and right, 68 bottom, 74 left and right, 91 bottom, 92 top left and top right, 92-93 bottom, 93 top left and bottom right, 103 inset, /© DC Thompson & Co. Ltd. 125 left, 127 bottom, /Private Eye 59 top; Pictorial Press 8-9, 56 bottom, 92 bottom left, 93 top right, 125 bottom right, 141; Popperfoto 12, 13, 20 left and right, 28, 29 left and right, 31 inset, 32 bottom, 36 top, 40 top left, 40-41 bottom, 51 top and bottom, 54, 55 left, 58 bottom, 60-61, 61 top, 62 bottom, 66, 67, 69, 78 inset, 78-79, 83, 87 bottom, 95, 112; Rex Features 41 bottom right, 80, 81, 87 top, 91 top, 100-101, 101 inset, 105, 122 inset, 128, 130 right; Derek Ridgers/LFI 7 bottom, 9 left, 110, 126, 132, 135, 138, 139; Topham both endpapers, 14-15, 16 main, 18 inset, 24 left and right, 30-31, 32 top, 34-35, 40-41 top, 43 bottom, 49, 56 top, 58 top, 63 left, 64-5, 70, 72 inset, 72-73, 73 inset, 77 top and bottom, 84-85, 86, 94 top, 96, 97, 98-99, 102, 103 left, 108, 113, 122-3; Michael Woodward Licensing © Alfred Gregory 7 top.

Ian Pape **Design**

Mike Evans **Editor**

Emily Hedges **Picture Research**

Tony Seddon **Design**